2012 and the End of the World

2012 and the End of the World

The Western Roots of the Maya Apocalypse

Matthew Restall
and
Amara Solari

ROWMAN & LITTLEFIELD PUBLISHERS, INC.
Lanham • Boulder • New York • Toronto • Plymouth, UK

Published by Rowman & Littlefield Publishers, Inc.
A wholly owned subsidiary of The Rowman & Littlefield Publishing Group, Inc.
4501 Forbes Boulevard, Suite 200, Lanham, Maryland 20706
http://www.rowmanlittlefield.com

Estover Road, Plymouth PL6 7PY, United Kingdom

Distributed by National Book Network

British Library Cataloguing in Publication Information Available

Library of Congress Cataloging-in-Publication Data Available

ISBN 978-1-4422-0609-0 (cloth : alk. paper)
ISBN 978-1-4422-0611-3 (electronic)

♾ ™ The paper used in this publication meets the minimum requirements of
American National Standard for Information Sciences—Permanence of Paper for
Printed Library Materials, ANSI/NISO Z39.48-1992.

Printed in the United States of America

To the Dads
and
to Babu, Onchito, and Fifty

Contents

Figures

Introduction

You Really Can Survive

*T*he countdown has begun to the end of the world. One can watch the final days tick away, second by second, on websites such as 2012-doomsday-predictions.com and chichen2012.org. There are hundreds of books on the 2012 phenomenon in print, warning us to prepare for the end or describing the new world that will follow. There is even a *Complete Idiot's Guide to 2012*, and survival kits can be purchased online; hurry while supplies—and the world—last.

The Internet is packed with blog chatter and websites devoted to revealing how the ancient wisdom of native peoples can "show us our future." For some, that future is an apocalyptic end of time, and thousands of people have booked their Doomsday vacations for the Grand Canyon, Stonehenge, Giza, Machu Picchu, or the Maya pyramids of Tikal and Chichén Itzá (figure 3 identifies the various Maya sites discussed in the book). An International Star Party series has already started at Copan, with the third (and final?) one scheduled for 2012. The looming apocalypse has become sufficiently well publicized and familiar for it to be lampooned by cartoonists (see figure 1).

For others, 2012 will herald the dawn of a new era. The end of the world, it seems, is not all bad. "2012 Is Real," warns another site with a countdown to the end; but not to worry, "you really can survive." John Major Jenkins, who has built a career on 2012, argues in

1. Bizarro Comic, by Dan Piraro, 2009.

dozens of books, essays, and interviews that the "end" is actually a beginning and a "new chance to recreate our world." On the website chichen2012.org, the link "know more about 2012" leads to a page with a button "Chichén Kids, upload your pics, participate and fun" (and, by the way, "It's Free").

Either way, doom or new dawn, there is something unnerving about watching the clock tick down to zero. Because the apocalyptic atmosphere in which we live is hard to avoid and end-of-the-world fever easy to catch, reassurances that we "really can survive" are not to be taken lightly. Furthermore, somewhere at the heart of all this "2012ology" (to borrow Jenkins's invention) are the Maya, the creators of one of the most impressive and revered civilizations in human history. The ancient Maya are not to be dismissed; maybe they were onto something.

Perhaps the Maya understood that natural disasters and human blunders will always threaten to destroy our world. After all, in the few years before 2012 the news has been full of horror stories of hurricanes, earthquakes, tsunamis, volcanoes, oil spills, global warming, nuclear stockpiles, and terrorist bombs. Is it not possible that centuries of stargazing led Maya priests to conclude that there is a pattern to the world's catastrophes? And, furthermore, that such a pattern may just culminate on the day 13.0.0.0.0 in the ancient Maya calendar that we call the Long Count —the day that is, in our calendar, December 21, 2012?

We begin our exploration of these questions, as most 2012 Doomsday prophecies do, with the Maya themselves. Our first chapter identifies the relevant Maya texts and images and explains what they say and how they seem to predict the world's demise. The second chapter then revisits and closely examines that evidence, as we analyze precisely what Maya priests and scribes did and did not prophesize. We offer a brief summary of Maya civilization, placing the topic of Maya prophecy in the larger context of whom the Maya were and how they viewed their world.

In our third chapter, we step away from the Maya to look elsewhere for answers—and find them on the other side of the Atlantic Ocean. We argue that it is Western—not Maya—civilization that contains what we call the millenarian mother lode. While Maya culture flourished in the Classic period (roughly the thousand years after AD 250), civilization in the Mediterranean and Western Europe increasingly embraced millenarian ideas. *Millenarianism* is the belief that an impending transformation will dramatically change society; *millennialism* expects such transformations to happen every thousand years; *chiliasm* (from the Greek *chilia*, "a thousand") is the specifically

Christian version of these beliefs, rooted in the biblical Book of Revelation; the destructive, end-of-world (or *eschatological*) manifestation of this transformation is often called the *Apocalypse*. Related terms will pop up later in the book. They are all, significantly, rooted in Western—not Mayan—languages.

Concepts of millenarianism and Apocalypse were deeply embedded within the cultures that were brought by Europeans to the Americas. Those ideas first of all reached Central Mexico, influencing the Aztecs and their neighbors in the early sixteenth century—a story we explore in our fourth chapter. Soon after, Spaniards invaded the kingdoms of the Maya, expanding the influence of Western culture into the cities and towns of Yucatan and Guatemala. In our fifth chapter, we explore how Christian notions of Doomsday and the Second Coming of Christ were easily appropriated, resulting in the cataclysmic narratives recorded by Maya scribes in the early colonial period. As the centuries passed, those narratives were viewed as an entirely Maya cultural phenomenon. They are often used as the basis for modern, popular interpretations of the Maya worldview and its prophecies.

Millenarian ideas were not restricted to premodern times. As Western civilization expanded across the Atlantic and moved into the modern era, apocalyptic ideas flourished in Europe and North America. Doomsday predictions never disappeared but simply jumped from one supposed end-of-world date to the next. In recent decades, no year has escaped prophesies of doom; regardless of when you are reading these words, you'll find online a prediction that the end is months, if not days, away.

In our sixth and final chapter, we outline how that larger phenomenon provides the context for the 2012 industry of tours, novels, guides, and books—including books like this one. We summarize the apocalyptic thread (2012 as the end) and the New Age thread (2012 as a utopian dawn), as well as fringe threads such as that of backup cataclysms. The chapter wraps up the evidence and arguments made in the preceding pages while also offering a brief summary of why the

2012 phenomenon has acquired such traction, and why, in human societies in general, there have been tendencies to embrace end-of-world predictions and fears.

In the end, do we unlock the mystery of 2012? Are we able to decode the secrets contained within ancient Maya wisdom, or the cosmic code of planetary movements, or the wisdom of the first Franciscan friars to preach in the New World? Our goal has been to take seriously a potentially silly topic. We ponder it with such purpose partly because it has been taken—and mistaken—so seriously by so many people and partly because the 2012 phenomenon has well-evidenced and fascinating historical roots that tell us something about our own civilization (as well as about ancient Maya civilization).

The origins of our book lie in a class, one that we are teaching at Pennsylvania State University in the fall of 2012. The course's goal is not simply to debunk 2012 myths or reassure undergraduates that the world will not end a few days after the semester does (and therefore there *is* a point to taking the final exam). Rather, the purpose of the class—and the book that arose out of our preparations for it—is to use 2012ology as a vehicle for combining the sources and methods of art history and history to explain the medieval, modern, and Maya contributions to the 2012 phenomenon, and thereby to find a fascinating tool with which to explore both Maya and Western civilizations.

This book, then, aims to explain what the 2012 fuss is all about. But we are not able to tell you whether the world is going to end in December 2012. To answer that question, you will just have to wait and see for yourself.

· 1 ·

The History of the End of the World

The Maya Prediction

"This is the history of the end of the world . . . the flood shall take place for the second time; this is the destruction of the world; this then is its end."

—from the colonial-period Yucatec Maya Book
of the Jaguar Prophet (*Book of Chilam Balam*)

"Predicted by the Mayans. Confirmed by science. Never before in history has a date been so significant to so many cultures, so many religions, scientists, and governments."

—from the promotional material for Sony
Pictures' *2012*

A t a remote point along the road that runs between two large towns in the Mexican state of Tabasco, a large concrete factory was built. The site was chosen for its access to stone and its location beside a highway. As far as anyone knew, or cared, nothing important lay there—no homes or valuable land. In the course of the factory's construction in the 1960s, a few man-made "hills" were bulldozed. By chance, several carved stone tablets were spotted among the rubble. They were saved, passed along to local officials, and eventually deposited in a Mexican museum as curiosities. The hieroglyphs could not

7

be read, and nobody could therefore be sure how old or how significant the stones might be.

In fact, the factory had been built upon an ancient Maya city, which was completely destroyed by the construction. Known to archaeologists today as El Tortuguero, the city was one of the most important smaller Maya sites in the region, subject to—and tied dynastically through its rulers—to the impressive city of Palenque (in today's neighboring state of Chiapas). The heyday of El Tortuguero seems to have been the seventh century; most of the carved monuments rescued from the site date from the reign of King Jaguar (Balam Ahau, AD 644–679).

The rescued monuments gathered dust for decades, until advances in Maya epigraphy (the decipherment of glyphs) inspired scholars to take a look at the long-forgotten, fragmented texts on the El Tortuguero stones. One of them was dubbed Monument 6 by Mayanists (Mayanists—the large international community of professional and amateur scholars who study the Maya, especially the ancient Maya, rather than their present-day descendents—give cities, buildings, and monuments names and numbers that tend to stick, even when the real names are later translated). Monument 6 had been broken up and its fragments scattered—four in a local Mexican museum, one in the Metropolitan Museum in New York, two in private collections, several other pieces lost. But when reconstructed, the glyphic text told not only the history of the king who had commissioned the monument; it seemed also to have calendrical significance.

Despite the damage and scattering and the loss of portions presumably destroyed by construction in the 1960s (if not before), Monument 6's glyphs are legible (drawn in figure 2). There are various ways to transcribe alphabetically and translate such a text; that caveat aside, the text can be read as: *Tzuh tzahoom uyuxlahuun pikta / Chan ahau ux unii / Uhtooma ili / Yeni yen bolon yookte kuh / Ta chak hohoyha.* The literal meaning of this might be: "The thirteenth one will end on 4 Ahau, the third of Uniiw. There will occur blackness and the descent of the Bolon Yookte' god to the red." Alternatively, the sec-

2. Monument 6 from El Tortuguero.

ond line might read: "There will occur a seeing, the display of the god Bolon Yookte' in a great investiture." A more idiomatic translation would read something like this: "The thirteenth calendrical cycle will end on the day 4 Ahau, the third of Uniiw, when there will occur blackness (or a spectacle) and the God of the Nine will come down to the red (or be displayed in a great investiture)."

The meaning is hardly clear, but with the application of some imagination the text can become an ominous warning, perhaps even an apocalyptic one. It has certainly become one of the sparks—by some accounts, *the* spark—that ignited the firestorm of the 2012 phenomenon. The Tortuguero text has been cited over and over since 1996 (when epigraphers Stephen Houston and David Stuart first published a translation of it) as the earliest example of Maya predictions of the world's end. This is partly because scholars initially speculated that the text might be a rare case of Classic Maya prophecy; subsequent retractions (to which we shall turn in the next chapter) fell on deaf ears. It is also partly because the passage's enigmatic and incomplete nature invites speculation: if we choose the first translation variant, black and red, the colors of darkness and blood, seem portentous; who is this god called Bolon Yookte', or the nine Yookte' gods, or the Gods of the Nine, and what catastrophe might his or their descent to Earth herald?

Above all, the Tortuguero passage has sparked controversy because the date to which it refers is approaching soon; in our calendar it is December 21, 2012 (sometimes given as 10 or 23, but usually 21, the winter solstice). In the Maya calendar, the date is a series of glyphs representing numbers; written out using our numbers, that date is 13.0.0.0.0. The zeros seem ominous, and the cycle whose end it marks is an impressively long one—5,126 years (more specifically 1,872,000 days or 5,126.37 years). That span of time takes us back to the dawn of human civilization—the beginnings of dynastic Egypt, the rise of Minoan civilization, the inception of Stonehenge, and perhaps too the dawn of the Maya world. Had the Maya calculated that settled human life existed within a specific time frame, a kind of cosmic, civilizational clock? And if so, is the tick of that clock getting louder and louder? Is the alarm about to go off?

~

It is tempting to comb through Maya literature to find clues as to what the Maya thought would happen on the day 13.0.0.0.0, and indeed many have succumbed to that temptation. Before we turn to look at some of those clues—in Maya carvings, ancient glyphs, and colonial-period alphabetic texts—a brief explanation of four core aspects of Maya civilization is necessary. These are political organization in the Maya region; the nature of Maya religion; the structure of the calendar; and creation mythology.

The Maya area was never politically unified. The peoples that we call "the Maya" comprised a civilization; they all shared a discrete set of cultural traits. But although they spoke dialects of the same family (the Mayan language family), all the Maya never spoke the same language. Nor did they ever recognize a common sense of identity or answer to a single ruler or dynasty. The region, stretching today from southern Mexico across Guatemala and Belize into Honduras, contained hundreds of polities (see figure 3). For thousands of years leading up to the Spanish invasion that began in the 1520s, small Maya kingdoms vied for regional control. Some built spectacular cities and conquered their neighbors. But no kingdom was able to dominate the whole Maya area, let alone any of its most populated and prosperous regions—such as northern Yucatan or highland Guatemala.

Maya rulers were kings, meaning that they held the top spot of an extremely steep social hierarchy. The position was seen as granted by the gods, a divine authority legitimated through familial bloodlines and religious roles. The king was a *kul ahau* (pronounced kool a-HOW, or *k'ul ajaw*), a "sacred ruler." An entire social class was devoted to religion—a priestly class, whose members were often close family members of the ruler or from other elite families. The religion they oversaw was complex and variable, composed of an elaborate pantheon of sacred beings, including both gods and deified ancestors.

The Maya pantheon was supported by a well-developed ritual tradition. Its purpose was to pay appropriate homage to the deities as a means of keeping the cosmos in order. Much like the ancient Greek pantheon, the Maya gods had humanlike personalities and engaged in

3. Map of the Maya area.

their own forms of revelry and social drama. In keeping with the regional nature of Maya identity, the gods were frequently localized; even when peoples from different ends of the Maya area worshiped the same deity, each viewed the deity as their own and claimed it had originated or been "born" in their home cities.

Maya calendrics is a complex topic, and a great deal has been written on it; what follows is a crude simplification. To the best of our knowledge, the Maya and their neighbors in southern Mexico developed solar (365-day) and lunar/gestational (260-day) calendars three to four thousand years ago. These were similar to our solar calendar (of 365-day years) and lunar calendar (our months). Probably around the second or third century BC a further calendar was developed, which Mayanists call the Long Count. This calendar, as its name suggests, viewed the passing of the years on a larger scale—rather like our centuries and millennia. The Long Count did not begin in the third century but was dated back to an earlier starting point: in our calendar, 3114 BC. The Maya counting system was vigesimal (a base of twenty, as opposed to our base of ten), and the number 13 was given particular importance (similar to the way we use 12). To simplify, this created the Long Count cycle mentioned above, stretching 5,126 years to our date 2012.

The Long Count cycle was composed of multiple minicycles, the shortest being a single day (the *kin*, also the word for "sun," roughly pronounced "keen"). Due to the Mesoamerican base-twenty counting system, the next cycle was composed of twenty days (the *uinal*, pronounced "WEE-nal"); eighteen of these *uinal* composed yet another cycle (the *tun*, pronounced like a short "toon"; in Yucatec Mayan, *tun* also meant "stone"). The *tun* totaled 360 days and approximated the solar year. Expanding further, twenty *tun* created the *katun* (about twenty years) and twenty *katun* created the four-hundred-year *baktun*. The calendar had the potential to expand infinitely; as we shall see shortly, some Maya cities advertized their mathematical skills by carving stone sculptures with Long Count dates reaching into the billions of years. Mayanists write out the Long Count as a series of numbers separated by periods running from right to left (the Maya themselves tended to write them in paired columns). For example, a date of 1 day, 12 *uinal*, 3 *tun*, and 2 *katun* would be written as 2.3.12.1.

One interpretation of the Long Count argues that it is by its very nature "predictive." In other words, it was not created by selecting a starting date and then counting forward, the way we count forward to 2012. Instead, the theory goes, the Maya selected a significant end date and then counted backwards. That end date—December 21, 2012—was found by calculating when in the future the various cycles of the Maya calendar would coincide on a winter solstice day. Such an interpretation privileges 2012, making it in a sense the key date within the entire complex edifice of Maya calendrics. There are other ways of interpreting the Long Count calendar—and we shall turn to them in the next chapter. But for now we leave you with the possibility that the Maya built that calendar specifically so they could know when its final day—perhaps *the* final day—would fall.

The final aspect of Maya civilization that needs to be briefly explained here is creation mythology. Our understanding of this mythology is based on two kinds of sources. One is ancient sources—glyphic texts and images in stone carvings, pottery paintings, and codices, mostly created in the thousand years before Spaniards began invading Maya kingdoms in the 1520s. The other is texts written alphabetically in Mayan languages during the three centuries of colonial rule that followed that invasion—most importantly a Quiché Mayan book called the *Popol Vuh* and a set of documents in Yucatec Mayan called the *Books of Chilam Balam* (both of which we shall examine in some detail below and in chapter 5). This may seem like a large body of evidence, but it covers variations across the Maya area and over thousands of years. So, again, simplification is in order.

The core idea relevant here is the Maya belief that the world was created repeatedly. Previous creations by the gods were not successful (because, for example, humans made of wood were not capable of worshiping their creators) and were therefore destroyed. The dominant metaphor of global destruction was a great flood. Conflict between the gods of the sky and of the underworld also tended to play a role in these destructions. The current creation is the third or fourth and is the age of maize (corn)—humans were made from maize, the crop that therefore sustains us.

In the contexts of the Long Count and creation mythology, the Tortuguero monument might be read as predicting that December 21, 2012, is the great milestone day, that the end of the great cycle will be accompanied by the next destruction of the world. Other ancient sites—some have argued—seem to support this impression, through the alignment of their buildings or through the artistic metaphors on their monuments or by the carved dates that proclaim the significance of other landmark days in the calendar.

One example is the beautiful ancient city of Izapa. The largest ancient site in what is today the Mexican state of Chiapas, Izapa's heyday was the half-millennium from 600–100 BC. Over two hundred stela, altars, and other carved stone monuments have been found at the site. Although the site is not technically a Maya one, and it lacks Long Count dates or any real glyphs at all, its monuments have been read as containing some of the earliest examples of calendrics and illustrations of Maya mythology. The dean of the spiritualist branch of 2012 predictions, John Major Jenkins, claims that Izapa's monuments allow us to decode "the secrets of Mayan sacred science"; the site is "the origin place of the 2012 calendar and the 2012 prophecy."

Jenkins argues that one set of buildings (the structures that archaeologists call the Group F Ballcourt) are aligned to the sunrise and sunset of the solstices; that the structures display galactic creation imagery (such as a solar deity paddling down the Milky Way in a canoe); and that Stela 25 encodes a cosmic map. The image on the stela (drawn in figure 4) shows a man holding a staff with a bird perched at the top. Several Mayanists have interpreted the bird as representing the Big Dipper. Others suggest that the figure is one of the Hero Twins, who in Maya creation mythology shoots a bird deity named Seven Macaw out of a tree with a blowgun (the anecdote is recorded in later Maya sources, on the Classic-period "Blowgunner Pot" and in the Quiché book, the *Popol Vuh*). According to the story, the Hero Twins had to shoot the macaw—also called the Principal Bird Deity by scholars—in order to usher in the transition from one world creation to the next.

4. Stela 25, Izapa.

There is also a caiman in the picture, bound head down. Jenkins sees the caiman's head as the head of the Milky Way; the "nuclear bulge" of the galactic center is just below his eye. The dots on the caiman's back are the stars of the Milky Way. The Polar Centre is at the top, with Seven Macaw (the Big Dipper) and the caiman aligned so as to represent the stars of the Milky Way as they appeared over Izapa at midnight on the summer solstice when the stela was erected (around the start of the third century BC). The result of all the Izapa evidence, says Jenkins, is "a dateless reference to an astronomical scenario" that points to the moments of creation, both at "era-3114 BC" and at "era-2012." We shall return to Izapa in the next chapter.

Another example of a monument with possible 2012 implications is Stela 63 in Copán, a spectacular Classic period Maya city in what is now Honduras. The stela highlights the day 9.0.0.0.0 as a calendrical milestone. The day is in the year AD 435, not 2012, in our calendar. But the implication is that if 9.0.0.0.0 matters, then 13.0.0.0.0 will matter as much, if not more. This is equivalent to commemorating Y1K in our calendar, thereby lending significance to Y2K.

A similar example is the monument in Cobá, a site in northeast Yucatan, which contains the oldest date recorded by the Maya. Cobá's Stela 1 does not limit the year count to five places (13.0.0.0.0 is a five-place count, 2012 is a four-place count). The Maya scribe counted back twenty-four places to carve a year that consists of twenty thirteens and four zeros. That is a date about a billion years larger than 13.7 billion BC, which is the age that astrophysicists currently assign to the universe. This may have merely been an act of "computational virtuosity" (as Mayanist Prudence Rice puts it), an exercise in showing off what could be done with the mathematics of the Long Count. Or the Maya elite at Cobá may have been demonstrating how the calendar was the formula that could be used to decode time, its numerical logic revealing when the universe was created and when each successive creation of the world and its humans occurred—and would occur.

Yet another example is a stunning stone carving at Quiriguá, known as Stela C (see figures 5 and 6). The large hieroglyphs on the surface of Stela C clearly feature the date 13.0.0.0.0. Quiriguá, in southeast Guatemala, was a midsized Maya city that was occupied for about a thousand years (from roughly 200 to 1200). Its history was intertwined with that of nearby Copán, to which it was subject until a successful revolt in 738. The kings of Quiriguá commissioned an impressive number of stone sculptures of various kinds, including the tallest stone monuments, or stelae, in the Americas. Some of the most important of these were carved under the rule of Cauac Sky (more accurately, K'ak' Tiliw Chan Yoaat).

King from 724 to 785, it was Cauac Sky who attacked Copán, captured its ruler, and had him executed in Quiriguá's main plaza. It

5. Stela C (south side) at Quiriguá, carved in 775.

6. Stela C (east side) at Quiriguá, carved in 775.

was also under Cauac Sky, in 775, when Stela C was erected. Its purpose was to commemorate and promote the divinity and legitimacy of the king by linking his reign to the creation of the cosmos. On the south side of the stela the king himself appears in full war regalia, wearing a military headdress and anklets (figure 5).

The stela's opposite side (the north side) was carved to represent an anthropomorphic being, some kind of composite elderly human-tree creature, which anthropologist Matthew Looper suggests is symbolic of his divine patronage of one of the cycles of the 365-day calendar. The deity raises one foot as if in dance, while the Principle Bird Deity perches above his head and umbilical cords flow to create the pattern of the universe. The west side is a long, hieroglyphic inscription that refers to a dedication ceremony made by an earlier king in 455 (we know this was not the first king, but Cauac Sky may have claimed him as a dynastic founder).

Finally, the east side of the stela, the most important for our story, relates the Maya mythological tale of the most recent creation, recording it as taking place in 13.0.0.0.0—not the future such date, but the past one, the zero date of the Long Count, 3114 BC. Either seen in their surviving state as stone carvings or drawn (figure 6), the glyphs that inscribe this date exemplify the combined impact of Maya art and calendrics; the conjunction of creativity and knowledge, beauty and intellect, compel us to see meaning in this so-called Creation Text. "The tripod is revealed, three stones are bundled, they place a stone, Jaguar Paddler, Stingray Paddler," reads the text, following the lengthy recording of the date.

> It happened at First Five Sky, Jaguar Throne Stone, he plants a stone, [unnamed god], it happened at [unnamed city], Snake Throne Stone, and then it happened, he bundled a stone. . . .

Continuing in this vein, the Quiriguá glyphs use the metaphor of the three hearth stones traditionally placed in Maya homes to describe the creation of the world; by referencing them as throne stones, Cauac Sky is also telling his subjects that his kingship is rooted in that same moment of creation—all the way back in 13.0.0.0.0 (3114 BC).

Cauac Sky's kingly ego was impressive indeed; in one stone monument, he tied his rule to the creation of the universe, the creation of the world, and the origins of the city's divine dynasty. So how does this relate to the end of the world? Arguably, by linking his reign to creation, Cauac Sky also evokes destruction, the absence of the world before its creation, and the possibility of future such cycles of destruction and creation.

What did the Maya think happened at the moment of world destruction and recreation? One possible answer is found on the final page of one of the few surviving Maya codices. The Dresden Codex, a bark-paper book created by a group of highly skilled Maya scribes in the fourteenth century, details the movements of the moon and planets and the resulting calendrical cycles. These all appear to culminate with a large caiman vomiting water from the sky (see figure 7). The image is a disturbing one, seeming to illustrate the destruction of the world in a great flood. Three great channels of water spew from the caiman. The glyphic text refers to the old goddess Chac Chel, who is pouring water from a jar in the center of the painting. The god Chac, painted black, crouches menacingly below, wielding weapons of destruction.

An apocalyptic interpretation of the final page of the Dresden Codex is especially compelling because the legend of the Great Deluge or the Flood appears elsewhere in Maya sources—indeed, in other parts of Mesoamerica (the larger civilizational area of which Maya civilization was a part). In Aztec creation mythology, for example, the fourth and most recent destruction and recreation of the world took the form of the Flood. This is also how the current world is created in the Quiché Maya narrative in the *Popol Vuh*; the humans made of wood are all swept away by the gods in the Flood. As Diego de Landa, a Franciscan friar in sixteenth-century Yucatan, was told by

7. *The Invocation of the Gods and the Grand Deluge*, from the Dresden Codex.

local Maya: previously *el mundo fue destruido por el diluvio*, "the world was destroyed by the Flood."

In the *Books of Chilam Balam* (Books of the Jaguar Prophet), a set of texts written in alphabetic Maya in colonial-period Yucatan, the flood is brought on by a battle between deities. The two main protagonists were the God of the Thirteen (Oxlahuntiku, god of the sky, which had thirteen levels), and the God of the Nine (Bolontiku, god of the underworld, which had nine levels). At one time, probably scores of towns and villages across Yucatan maintained their own version of these books—which contained a mixture of history and mythology, prophecy and calendrics, herbal lore and medicinal remedies—although less than a dozen survive today. The surviving manuscripts date from the late eighteenth century but contain material copied repeatedly from previous centuries, some of it likely transferred from glyphic books (codices) painted before the arrival of the alphabet and Christianity.

The books from Chumayel, Tizimín, and Maní feature almost identical versions of the creation myth that includes the flood story. It is *u kahlay cab tu kinil,* "the history of the world in those days," declares the Chumayel version, which goes on to describe the epic battle between Oxlahuntiku and Bolontiku. After Oxlahuntiku wins,

> There was one rush of rain, one sharp burst of rain, as when the Archangel of the corn field came. The sky was stormy; it was stormy on earth too. The four gods spoke/stood, the four *bacabs* [rain gods], causing this destruction. Then when the destruction of the earth was finished, it [the earth] was settled, so that Kan Xib Yui [a bird god] can put it in order, and the white *imix* [ceiba] tree speak/stand to the north. It speaks/stands there as a pillar of the sky and also as a sign of the destruction of the world; this white ceiba tree speaks/stands in support. Then the black ceiba tree spoke/stood too, where the black-bellied *pidzoy* [bird] lives. Then the yellow ceiba tree spoke/stood too, a sign of the destruction of the world; there the yellow-bellied *pidzoy* lives, and there sits Kan Xib Yui and the yellow *oyal mut* [bird]. Then the blue green ceiba tree spoke/stood too, in the center. It sits, placed there, as a record of the destruction of the world.

What is going on here? Is this a Maya description of Doomsday? In a way, it is. The passage uses creation mythology and the annual coming of the rains as metaphors for each other; a violent spring storm is like the Flood, destroying the world, but also leads to its re-creation as symbolized by trees and birds. The trees both speak and stand (the scribe uses *ual*, which is both *u al*, "it speaks" and *ual*, "to set up, stand"). They speak in testimony, as "signs" or symbols, of the world's "destruction," and they stand as pillars supporting the sky and thus maintaining the world from another destruction. These myth-trees, color-coded and oriented to the cardinal directions, are like Maya stelae—planted deep in the soil, they both stand and speak of the history of the (local) world.

The trees are called *imix che* for a reason. The term is a way of referring to a ceiba tree, which was symbolic and significant to the Maya in a similar way to how we see the oak tree. But there is a further reason: the Flood occurs at the end of the *katun*, or twenty-year cycle, named 13 Ahau, and in the calendar the day following *ahau* is named *imix*. The trees are thus more than symbols of the world's destruction; they are named for the day after. They are, in the end, more about *The Day After Tomorrow* than about *2012*.

However it is read, the *Chilam Balam* text seems to be a different version of the Flood story presented visually at the end of the Dresden Codex. But what of the caiman whose role is so vivid in the codex? Sure enough, in the version of the book from the towns of Maní and Tizimín, the caiman does make an appearance. This caiman, called Itzam Cab Ain, Lizard Earth Caiman, is not in the sky (as in the Dresden Codex image) but holds up the earth; and he does not spew water (as in the Dresden) but must be slain for the destructive flood to be complete:

> Then Itzam Cab Ain is born. The day is cut at dawn, so that the sky is split and the land revealed. And thus begins the book of Oxlahuntiku. Then a great flooding of the earth takes place; then up rises the great Itzam Cab Ain; the end of the telling, the composition of the *katun*; that flood will be the end of the telling of the *katun*. But Bolontiku did not wish it. So he cut the throat of Itzam Cab Ain, who carries the land on his back.

In another passage, the caiman is absent; but the flood seems to accompany an apocalyptic ending to the *katun* cycle:

> Here is when it shall end, the telling of the *katun*; that is what is given by God; the flood shall take place for the second time; this is the destruction of the world; this then is its end.

This brings us back to Tortuguero, and the connection is potentially ominous. "There will occur black . . ." predict the glyphs on Monument 6; the weapon-wielding Chac in the Dresden image is painted black. The Tortuguero text continues, "The Gods of the Nine will descend to the red . . ."; a manifestation of this god heralds the destruction of the world in the Flood, according to the *Chilam Balam* narratives. Named Bolon Yookte' K'uh (or Bolonyooktiku) in the Tortuguero glyphs, he is Bolontiku in the *Chilam Balam* texts. The name is the same: *bolon* is "nine"; *ku* is "god"; the syllables in between are, loosely speaking, locatives, with *yook* indicating a plurality. Bolontiku is the God of the Nine, the god of the nine levels of the underworld, and his presence in 2012 is surely not a good sign.

One translator of the *Chilam Balam* literature, the late Munro Edmonson, has argued that some of the passages we have quoted above are from a celebration of the cycle that ended in 1618, a *Ceremonial of the Baktun* that took place in the Yucatec capital city of Merida. In the words of Edmonson and his Mayanist colleague Victoria Bricker, "This extravaganza was in honor of the fact that the date marked the beginning of an even baktun: 12.0.0.0.0." Of the twenty separate ceremonies, or what these scholars dub "acts of the drama," the third is the "Cycle-ending ceremony." This features the battle described above, in which the God of the Nine defeats and sacrifices the God of the Thirteen; the image of the deity of the underworld rising up and slaughtering the deity of the heavens has clearly apocalyptic overtones.

According to Edmonson's reading, the ritual featured "the millennial words here / For the examination / Of the Mayan people here / Who may know / How they were born / And settled the land / Here / In this country." For Edmonson, the passage reflected the fact that "competent hieroglyphic writing probably lasted" into the seventeenth century, "and the Long Count calendar certainly did." Here, then, were the Maya seeming to use formal "millennial" speech and ritual to mark the moment when the last *baktun* of four hundred years ended and the next one began? What is that next *baktun*? It is ours, and it ends in December 2012.

∿

Lay hay cabile lay tun cu dzocole: "this is the destruction of the world; this then is its end." The meaning of such a phrase seems clear; indeed, all these Maya texts and images seem to add up to something significant. Dates carved in stone monuments, images of Apocalypse, narratives of cyclical catastrophe, all appear to support the notion that the Maya knew that the end was nigh—and they had figured out exactly when it would happen. Even so, without the Tortuguero monument and its specific citing of the winter solstice day in 13.0.0.0.0, 2012ology and the whole phenomenon might not have developed. Had one of those bulldozers in the 1960s moved a few feet one way or another, we might have missed the warning.

· 2 ·

They Deserve Better

The Maya Evidence

"The Mayans, who were good-enough astronomers and timekeepers to predict Venus's position 500 years in the future, deserve better than this."

—*New York Times*, 11/16/2009

"2012 has gained the status of an icon, a cultural symbol, to be used and often abused for purposes that have nothing to do with its origins and the intentions of its creators."

—John Major Jenkins, *The 2012 Story*

*D*id the Maya try to warn us that the end was nigh?

To answer this question, we should begin where the first chapter began: with Monument 6 from El Tortuguero. Does that text tell us that the world will end "when the thirteenth cycle ends," that the apocalypse will come when "the God of the Nine comes down to the red"?

In fact, the Tortuguero monument tells us no such thing. Its uniqueness and importance lie in the fact that it cites the date at the end of the Long Count. But, ironically, therein lies its very weakness as a source for Doomsday prediction. In other words, because it is unique, its potential as prophecy is not reinforced by other Maya texts; when it is placed in the context of other such texts, its significance weakens. Monument 6 tells us very little of what will happen on December 21, 2012, partly because it is a broken fragment, partly because that was not its purpose. Thus, when we turn to the larger context of Maya texts for clues to better understanding Monument 6, its supposed millenarian significance fades.

Let us explain. When the Tortuguero passage was first tentatively deciphered in 1996, there were no monuments from other Maya cities that were similar enough to the Tortuguero's Monument 6 to be helpful. But since then, two Maya texts of a similar genre have been uncovered and translated. One is dated 593 from Naranjo, the other is dated 677 from La Corona (both in Guatemala). All three texts are on stone markers dedicating the completion of a new building. All three provide the dates of that moment of dedication but also cite future dates that mark the end of calendrical cycles. The Naranjo text cites 10.0.0.0.0 (830 in our calendar); the La Corona one cites a series of dates culminating in 9.13.0.0.0 (692) (see figure 8, Naranjo on the left, La Corona on the right).

These are symbolically pleasing, round, cycle-completing dates, like 13.0.0.0.0—or like our Y2K. The La Corona text, like Tortuguero's monument, also evokes a thirteenth cycle—a cycle that, as we have seen, had a cultural resonance among the Maya similar to our millennia. Neither of the Guatemalan monuments leap as far forward as Tortuguero's 13.0.0.0.0 (2012), and the purpose of the future dates is not clear. But there is nothing in the dedicatory texts to suggest the prediction of disaster. On the contrary, one might more reasonably speculate that the intent was something like "Built in 1900, this will still stand in 2000." The alternative interpretation of the text presented in the previous chapter—which has the God of the Nine seen and displayed "in a great investiture"—further supports this reading of the monument as dedicatory, not prophetic.

That does not sound very ominous, and it isn't; indeed, its spirit is arguably the opposite from apocalyptic, invoking longevity and permanence rather than ephemerality and predetermined destruction.

8. Left: Portion of Naranjo Altar 1; right: Portion of La Corona Panel 2.

A dozen years after he and David Stuart first translated the Tortuguero glyphs and speculated that they might be prophetic, Stephen Houston offered a "mea culpa and a rectification"—the text, he admitted, "had nothing to do with prophecy."

But it was too late. The imaginary cat was already out of the bag. The 2012ologists Geoff Stray and John Major Jenkins protested that scholars had been deliberately downplaying Tortuguero's implications for years; because of the professional Mayanists' fear of the 2012 "monster" and their "cliqueish" "closed shop" mentality, "a logical deduction of great relevance was ignored, or withheld." Responding to the evidence that the Tortuguero text was in part a building dedication, Jenkins observed that the Maya viewed "house" and "cosmos" as metaphorically linked. The point, broadly speaking, is valid and interesting, but sometimes a building is just a building.

~

The Maya prediction of the world's end is based on their Long Count cycle. Without the Long Count, there is no 2012. We introduced the Long Count briefly in the previous chapter, but to analyze the 2012 evidence fully, four aspects of this calendar need to be examined in more detail. First, if the end date of 2012 is determined by the placing of the start date, how was that start date selected? Second, how do we know that the Maya Long Count date of 13.0.0.0.0.0 is December 21, 2012, in our calendar? Third, how widely used and recognized was the Long Count among the Maya? And fourth, do we know what the Maya thought would happen, in calendrical terms, *after* 2012?

Much of the discussion surrounding the significance the Maya supposedly attached to the year 2012 ignores this obvious question: if 2012 is the end of the great Long Count cycle of 5,126 years, how did the Maya figure out when that cycle began? In other words, how did they pick the Long Count's year zero? If the Long Count developed the way our long calendar did—through a series of idiosyncratic decisions, mistakes, and coincidences—then is the approach to 2012 merely "a precisely arbitrary countdown" (as Stephen Jay Gould called the march to Y2K)? In the previous chapter, we mentioned the theory that the Long Count was by its very nature "predictive"—that its cycle was determined by its end date, not its start. This theory was proposed by a few Mayanists decades ago, and 2012ologists such as José Arguelles and Jenkins have made it a foundation stone to their entire 2012 positions. However, it is not widely accepted among Mayanists today, as there is no evidence to support such a theory; it is an intriguing speculation, but not one supported by any other text or image among Maya sources.

Instead, two other possibilities are more likely and more widely accepted. In the calendars used in the world today, the zero date tends

to refer to a specific historical event, often with a religious significance (such as the birth year of Christ or the year Muhammad left
Mecca) or a political one (such as the Japanese calendars' reference to
Japan's mythical founding by the Emperor Jimmu or the reign of the
current emperor). The zero date of the Long Count is, in our calendar, 3114 BC. So did something happen in the Maya area in 3114
BC—politically, culturally, or astronomically—that is reflected in the
Long Count? That is too far back for there to be any visual or textual
record of events in the Maya world, nor do later texts refer to anything in particular happening in that year. Furthermore, astronomers
tell us that 3114 BC was not an especially significant date in terms of
the night sky or planetary alignment, so we cannot look to the ancient
skies for a satisfactory explanation.

What about the circumstances surrounding the initial use of the
Long Count dates, the first time they were carved into stone? Do we
know when that occurred, and does that moment offer any clues?
The short answer is no. But the earliest examples of Long Count dates
recorded come from the first century BC, and Mayanists plausibly
speculate that it was created earlier, perhaps a century or two earlier.
Archaeoastronomer Anthony Aveni and other scholars propose that if
the Long Count was conceived in the second or third century, the
Maya may have counted back from the nearest round date—such as
7.6.0.0.0 (236 BC). In other words, they imagined that the world
they lived in had been created a few thousand years earlier and dated
that creation in order to give the current year a satisfying trio of zeros
in a five-place Long Count date. They then structured that count
around the number 13, pinning the end of the cycle a couple of thousand years in the future and placing themselves more or less in the
middle.

This, in our view, is the most credible explanation. In terms of
2012 predictions, the implications are resounding. Simply put, the
element of arbitrariness in the placing of the Long Count is such that
it alone—all other evidence aside—undermines the credibility of
Maya-based 2012 prophecies.

Second, how do we know that the Long Count date of 13.0.0.0.0 is our December 21, 2012? The answer is that we can be fairly certain, but not 100 percent sure. Many scholars have devoted energy to the question of calendrical correlation, and there are at least twenty-seven fully developed correlations, each giving a slightly different date in our calendar for 13.0.0.0.0. The most widely accepted correlation is called GMT, after the Mayanists who contributed to it (Goodman, Martínez, and Thompson). One could argue that there is a smidgeon of reasonable doubt regarding the GMT correlation. On the other hand, today's leading Mayanists endorse it fully; as Michael Coe persuasively comments, "there is now not the slightest chance that these three scholars were not right."

Third, how widely used was the Long Count? Although it was the grandest cycle in Maya calendrics, it was neither the first nor the last calendar. That is, the Maya developed and used their shorter calendars (the solar year and the 260-day lunar/gestational calendar) for hundreds of years before the Long Count was invented. And they continued to use those other calendars for centuries after the Long Count gradually faded from usage in the ninth century. Its demise was a symptom of the decline of divine kingship. The Long Count and the institution of the sacred ruler, the *kul ahau*, rose, flourished, and fell together. Both had appropriated religion and time for political purposes. The great stone-carved dates had glorified the great kings; without the sacred rulers, the counting and recording of those days had no reason to exist. The last recorded Long Count inscription dates from AD 910—some six centuries before Spaniards arrived in Mesoamerica. Thus the Long Count was not extinguished by Europeans but was slowly abandoned by the Maya themselves.

Fourth, what did the Maya believe would happen to the Long Count *after* 2012, or 13.0.0.0.0? If that date marked the world's end, did the count likewise simply end? There are various possible answers to that question, based on the varying ways in which Long Count dates were recorded on Classic monuments. But none of those variants suggest that 2012 was merely a terminal date. If the Maya of

Quiriguá were still recording dates today, for example, they would see the end of the cycle as simultaneously the start of the next one. The Long Count actually records days, so December 21, 2012, is both 13.0.0.0.0 and simply zero (or 0.0.0.0.0). December 22 will be 1 (or 0.0.0.0.1). After twenty days, the date will be 0.0.0.1.0, and so on.

For the creators of Stela 1 at Cobá—the monument with the twenty-four place date recording billions of years—the end of the cycle on December 21, 2012, would have marked a transition from a five-place count to a six-place one. Thus they would have rewritten 13.0.0.0.0 as 1.0.0.0.0.0, with the next day (December 22) as 1.0.0.0.0.1. Time would not have ended but expanded as it marched on indefinitely.

The Maya elite who carved dates in the beautiful Classic city of Palenque (in today's Chiapas, Mexico) likewise viewed time—and their world—as existing before and after the Long Count cycle in which they lived. One glyphic text, from the Temple of the Inscriptions, makes the reign of the great king K'inich Janaab' Pakal (known more popularly as Pakal) seem all the more momentous by noting that the eightieth calendar round (or calendrical cycle) anniversary of his accession to the throne will take place eight days after the end of the 8,000-year Long Count cycle called the *pictun*. This bit of Maya numerological fun records two days in October AD 4772.

Or take the glyphic text, for example, that appears on the building that Mayanists call the Temple of the Cross (figure 9). It records the birth of a woman and a man seven to eight years (in 3122 and 3121 BC) *before* the creation of the long cycle. The creation itself is momentous but not accompanied by cataclysm or destruction. This is our idiomatic translation of approximately the first third of one of the texts from this Palenque temple. It records the birth of the woman shortly before the dawn of the new cycle and the arrival of a new deity shortly afterwards:

On 12.19.13.4.0 [December 7, 3121 BC], First Lady Sek was born. Five months and eight years after she was born, the era

9. The Temple of the Cross, Palenque.

was wrapped up; the 13 cycles of 400 years were completed on 13.0.0.0.0 [August 13, 3114 BC]. A year, 9 months, and 2 days after the face of the new era was revealed, Hun Ye Nal Chac appeared in the sky; on 13.0.1.9.2 [February 5, 3112 BC] he dedicated the Raised-Sky House, the Eight Chac House was its holy name, the Home of the North.

This passage has been variously translated and analyzed, and the specific mythology it introduces—the ancestral and divine origins of the Palenque king that had the temple built—is not our primary concern. What matters to us here is the fact that the birth of two mythical ancestral beings bridges the transition from the previous Long Count era to the new one. The date 13.0.0.0.0.0, the day that starts the long cycle to end in 2012, is not a day of Apocalypse. It is simply a resetting of the calendrical clock, a milestone to mark time in the distant past. In that past, birth and creation, not death and destruction, were the important events.

Dennis Tedlock, a leading scholar of Maya literature, argues that a goddess is the most common Maya metaphor for the dawn of a new era. In the previous chapter we discussed the final page of the Dresden Codex and its depiction of the Flood; in doing so, we deliberately downplayed the fact that the codex is overwhelmingly not about endings but about cycles (or, put another way, every ending is also a new beginning).

The codex consists of astronomical tables and almanacs, charting the movements of the moon and of Venus, and placing agricultural seasons within the context of planetary movements. Deities act as metaphors for everything, from the planets to the dates of the 260-day calendar. The deity that perhaps best signifies the dawning of a new era is called Ix Ahau Na (or Ix Ajaw Nah), Lady House. Her "house" is in the sky, around Virgo. She is depicted in the codex sitting on her throne in the vault of the sky, receiving offerings (see figure 10).

Lady House in the Dresden text, like First Lady Sek in the Palenque text, is not a metaphor of doom; on the contrary, these women represent dawn, not destruction. In an alphabetic Maya text from colonial Yucatan (called the *Ritual of the Bacabs*) the equivalent goddess is called Ix Kin Sutnal. Literally meaning "she of the sun's turn" or "the day's turn," we might call her Lady Returning Sun. In the Paris Codex, her animal avatar is a frog taking the sun in his mouth; in the Madrid Codex, she is a frog jumping or diving in the rain. Her time of the year is March, when the rains begin, the frogs appear and start to sing, and corn is planted. As Tedlock puts it, the day 1.0.0.0.0.1 "should be a good time for planting, and for making new starts of all kinds."

∽

The Long Count thus makes for a very shaky foundation for Maya 2012 predictions. But there still remains the issue of Maya millenarianism. By quibbling over the calendar, are we missing the larger point? Did the Maya know that the world in which we live had a limited life span, and are we being imprudent to ignore that knowledge?

10. *Ix Ahau Na* (Lady House) from the Dresden Codex.

The ancient Maya left us an extraordinarily rich array of build-ings, stone carvings, paintings, pottery, hieroglyphic texts, books, and other evidence of their cultural accomplishments. Most of this mate-rial—certainly the most studied and celebrated structures, monu-ments, and artifacts—comes from the millennium between AD 200 and 1200. But the complete record of Maya civilization stretches from the fifth century BC up to the present day. If we look at two millennia of that evidence, from the fifth century BC up to the eve of the sixteenth-century European invasion, what impression are we given? Specifically, what seems to have been the primary concerns of the Maya who wrote, painted, carved, designed, and built?

Ask ten Mayanists that question and you will get ten different answers. That caveat aside, we suggest the following six concerns. The first was the fertility of the earth and its agricultural cycles; this is hardly surprising, as Maya society was agrarian and the diet was based on corn and other crops (little meat was available to them). The second was the dovetailing of the natural and supernatural worlds; in a sense, they were one world, occupied by kings, ancestors, shamans, people, animals, and the pantheon of gods (introduced in chapter 1) —all dependent for their survival upon each other.

The third was the permanence of place, viewed in highly local terms. There was never an empire that united the Maya, never a language or common sense of identity (again, as introduced in chapter 1). Politics was regional, relations between city-states frequently violent, and cities developed highly local identities; one of the remarkable features of Maya architecture is how distinct and different every major site is from the others. The city was not a city in our sense of the word; its residents lived village lives rather than urban ones. But the pyramids, palaces, and temples of the city were seen as deeply rooted in that location, as permanently a part of the fabric of the world as the city's trees and whatever mountains or rivers lay near it.

The fourth was time—the pace of its passing, its observation in the natural world and in the night sky, its measurement and its recording. Time was central to agricultural concerns and the need to control as much as possible the cycles of fertility and growth. The grasp of time was central to the legitimacy claims of kings and priests. Time was, to be sure, a source of anxiety, but it was also the most constant aspect of life on earth; it might seem to pass slowly at times, fly by at others, but the Maya understood that in reality its passage was unfailingly uniform.

The fifth concern was aesthetics, how things looked and should look. One could argue that the entire vast corpus of Maya art and architecture was a millennia-long exploration of beauty, an endless investigation into visual sensibility. None of the Mayan languages seem to have had, or have, a word for "art"; but, as prominent Mayanist art historian Mary Ellen Miller has put it, "The ancient Maya world was a world of Maya art."

The sixth and final concern of the Maya, we suggest, was humor and play. Every Maya city had at least one ball court, and the ball game is widely illustrated in Maya art. Beyond the ball game, comedy and play of various kinds featured strongly in Maya life. Comic themes in Maya art, many of which we can barely begin to grasp, hint at a whole world of mockery, celebration, and laughter. Maya art is full of humor, its sculpture and mythology is packed with jokes—ranging from the goofy to the dark, albeit with nuances and punch lines that Mayanists have yet to decipher.

Nowhere in this set of concerns is there a preoccupation with the end of the world, the end of time, apocalypse, extinction, or even an exceptional or unusual focus on death. The most egregious misrepresentation (among many) in Mel Gibson's 2006 movie *Apocalypto* was the styling of the Maya as obsessively and sadistically morbid. Maya life was not overshadowed by death or a fear of the end of time. They did not develop notions of redemption or salvation based on the arrival or return of a leader or deity. To be sure, their complex grasp of calendrics featured a well-developed sense of cyclicity—the cycles of life and death, of planetary movements, of the agricultural seasons. Furthermore, this included an interest in how catastrophic events, from natural disasters to political violence, might repeat themselves according to similar cyclic rhythms. But almost all the evidence for Maya interest in the cycles of disaster dates from after the Spaniards invaded and introduced Christianity. In general, the Maya were simply not focused on ideas that we would call millenarian or apocalyptic.

Popular perceptions of the Maya tend to incorporate outdated misreadings of the Maya past—with the Maya often conflated with the Aztecs and reduced to a millenarian essence. An example is figure 11, drawn from a graphic that appeared in Boston.com. In the original graphic, the "Mayan Empire" label was accompanied by a caption headed "Collapse of the Maya. Before the year 1000." The caption explained that "the Classic Maya built a powerful society with sophisticated cities and a rich cultural life. War, overpopulation, deforestation, and soil erosion helped hasten its end." The illustrative images

11. Redrawing of an educational graphic from boston.com.

are a pyramid from the Classic Maya city of Tikal and a polychrome rendering of the central portion of an Aztec sculpture called the Calendar Stone (or Sun Stone).

The impression given is one of political centralization, ominous calendrical wisdom, imperial hubris, and millennial collapse. The creator of the original graphic and caption should not be blamed for this; on the contrary, it reflects Mayanist scholarship of decades ago and the persistent popular impression of the Maya today. The point is that such an image is outdated and misleading. The Calendar Stone has nothing whatsoever to do with the Maya (see our discussion of it in chapter 4). There was never a "Mayan Empire," or even Maya empires. There was indeed a time of population loss and the abandonment of cities, but that process was a gradual one lasting centuries and only affecting specific regions of the Maya area. Mayanists debate whether the term *collapse* is appropriate to this process at all; either way, only by a great stretch of the millenarian imagination was there a sudden "collapse of *the* Maya" (our italics). They did not come to an end "before the year 1,000," nor did they live in anticipation of coming to an end in 2012.

∽

If the Maya did not have a well-developed sense of apocalypse, how did the notion of Maya millenarianism get attached to the Long Count cycle? The blame can largely be placed in the hands of early Mayanist scholars—somewhat ironically, as it is professional Mayanists who have more recently been trying to expose the myth of 2012 Maya predictions. Comments by early Mayanists created small snowballs that, over the years, picked up the flakes of amateur astronomers and Maya devotees, spiritualists and New Age writers, and the many heirs to the West's deep traditions of apocalyptic anticipation; the result is today's avalanche of Maya-based 2012 literature.

For example, in a 1957 study of the calendar dates of the Dresden Codex, pioneering Mayanist and astronomy professor Maud Makemson (1891–1977) remarked that "the completion of a Great Period of

13 b'ak'tuns [i.e., reaching the date 13.0.0.0.0] would have been of the utmost significance to the Maya." This and similar comments were cited over the successive decades and can be found now on websites such as Wikipedia. Makemson's breathless comments on "the astonishing scope of the Maya imagination and inventive powers" were very much a part of the tone of early Mayanism and remain central to the way in which the Maya "mystique" is perpetuated today.

Makemson represents well the foundations to the giddy relationship between Mayanism and 2012; she found Maya calendrics "awe-inspiring" and said enough along those lines to be used as fodder for 2012 prophecy speculation. But she knew full well that the Maya were not Apocalypse-oriented. In fact, she argued that the Maya "invented the Long Count, which was essentially a tally of days since a normal or zero date" in order to give each day a unique name; that is, *not* to highlight a vast cycle or "Great Period" but to deemphasize cyclicity and explore linear dating. Because the calendars invented earlier by the Maya were cycles, each day eventually repeated itself; the Long Count permitted a long-range linearity and unique dating (the way that adding 2012 to December 21 makes that day unique).

Another scholar whose views of 2012 illustrate the development of the phenomenon is Michael Coe. A prominent Mayanist since the 1960s, Coe's career spans the decades of the epigraphic break-through—the decipherment of Maya hieroglyphs—a story he documented to much acclaim in his book *Breaking the Maya Code*. In the first edition (1966) of his textbook, *The Maya*, his explanation of the calendar used the term *Armageddon*. It had been suggested, wrote Coe, that, "when the Great Cycle of the Long Count reaches completion . . . on the final day of the thirteenth" cycle, "our present universe will be annihilated."

But the glyphs could not be read back then, nor was there a reliable correlation that fixed the Maya day of possible Armageddon in our calendar. Coe suggested December 24, 2011; in the second edition (1980) of his textbook, that final day was given as January 11,

2013; the fourth edition (1983) of a rival textbook offered December 21, 2012; in his next edition (1984), Coe suggested December 23, 2012. But these contradictions did not mark any sort of controversy; the differences of opinion were part of the unfolding understanding of Maya writing and mathematics, with nobody arguing that ancient astronomers actually thought the world would end with the "Great Cycle." In other words, the goal was to try to correlate the calendars—an esoteric intellectual exercise—not to reveal the day of the Apocalypse.

A shift occurred in the 1990s; by Coe's sixth edition (1999) of *The Maya*, he had deleted all speculation about the end of the Long Count's cycle. In the fifteen years leading up to 2012, Mayanists either withdrew from the discussion or issued statements clarifying that the Maya had undoubtedly *not* predicted the world's end. What had changed?

Several factors converged to explain the emergence of 2012 as a Maya-based phenomenon. First, the steady decipherment of Maya writing since the 1970s led to a flurry of exhibitions and publications and helped spur archaeological work in more and more ancient Maya cities, bringing the Maya increasingly into the public consciousness. Second, the analysis of a few specific monuments for the first time—such as the 1996 reading of Tortuguero's Monument 6—drew attention to the notion of Maya calendrics as an apocalyptic puzzle to be solved. Third, the supposed final day of December 21, 2012—now fixed by the GMT correlation and Mayanist consensus as the end of the Long Count's Great Cycle—started to loom in the near future.

Fourth, another thread of intellectual speculation—primarily identifiable as New Age and spiritualist thinking—latched on to the Maya as a source of ancient wisdom. We return later (in chapter 6) to the New Age and spiritualist branch of 2012ology, the 2012 Gnostics (as Aveni calls them). For now, our interest is in how such writers have combined Maya sources with astronomy to advance 2012 ideas.

For example, in 1987 José Arguelles helped organize an international "Harmonic Convergence" event, based on the notion that an exceptional alignment of the planets would produce a millenarian moment in August of that year. Arguelles insists that, based on a convoluted reading of the Aztec calendar, 1987 was the start of the transformation. Its culmination, or galactic "beam end," will be on December 21, 2012; the Maya calendar, he claims, was aligned to predict and anticipate the galactic convergence. During the 1990s John Major Jenkins picked up this thread and explored it in great detail; his 1998 *Maya Cosmogenesis 2012* was the first book in this exploding genre of literature with the year 2012 in the title. The core notion developed by Jenkins—which he points out has been widely misread and abused and which is now scattered across the Internet—is that the galaxy, or even the universe, will be realigned or altered in a way that will either usher in a new and improved era (Jenkins's position) or destroy earth. The Maya, with their famous stargazing skills, are credited with anticipating this event.

Most versions of this theory by Jenkins and others center on precession. Precession is the astronomical term that refers to how the sun becomes gradually aligned with the Milky Way. The Earth's axis of rotation shifts a little each year, resulting in a slight difference between the solar year (how long it takes us to revolve around the sun) and the stellar year (how long it takes us to line up with the stars). This phenomenon can be observed without modern technology; it was spotted as early as 128 BC by the Greek astronomer Hipparchus.

It is possible, therefore—perhaps likely—that the Maya were aware of the precession. Jenkins insists that "there is in fact a great deal of evidence that the ancient Maya were aware of precession," although Mayanists argue that there is nothing in ancient or colonial texts to suggest that they actually recorded or tracked it. Anthony Aveni, in a rather brilliant summary of the evidence, concludes that the Maya "certainly could have detected precession" but that "there is no evidence to date to support the case that they calculated the cycle, much less even perceived precession as a cyclic phenomenon." Even if we accept the claim that the Maya did try to track it, the precession cycle is about 26,000 years and cannot be predicted through observation to a specific date; at best, one can predict the alignment will occur within a period of a few centuries, perhaps one century, but not one year—let alone one day.

What of the cosmic map in Stela 25 at Izapa, the significance of which Jenkins ties to his argument that the Maya were well aware of precession? Jenkins asserts that the Izapans—and thus the Maya, although Izapa was not a Maya city—knew that the precession's significance was not just astronomical but spiritual. The next precession will create an inner alignment in us all, allowing us to "reconnect with our cosmic heart and eternal source"; Izapa reveals that its ancient creators knew this.

Jenkins's take on Izapa is appealing, makes for good reading, and should not be dismissed out of hand; but ultimately it is not persuasive. To conclude that the Maya associated the precession with the next world creation is to make an enormous interpretive leap. The image on Stela 25 may be a cosmic map, and it may indicate a galactic alignment. But the argument is speculative, not substantiated with either internal or contextual evidence.

Furthermore, the Maya were not mapmakers; cartography was one of the few expressions of artistic and spatial representation that the Maya did *not* develop. Amid the vast corpus of ancient Maya art and writing, there is not a single case of a map—not in our sense of the term, in the sense meant by the reading of Stela 25 as a map. When the Maya do start making maps it is in the early colonial period; the result is a handful of Spanish-influenced, micropatriotic maps, centered on the town of origin and reflecting the highly localized identity of the sixteenth-century Maya (figure 12 is a 1557 example, the "round map" from Mani, in northern Yucatan). These were a far cry from star maps; in Aveni's words, they are "*loco*-centric, not *helio*-(sun) or *galacto*-centric."

Finally, even if, for the sake of argument, we were to accept Stela 25 as a unique example of a star map, there is nothing in this image—or any of the other two hundred images from Izapa—that predicts or even suggests a future event. Nor is there any mention of

12. Gaspar Antonio Chi, The Mani Land Treaty Map, 1557.

a distant future date, or even any Long Count dates, let alone 2012. We too would like to think that over two thousand years ago the builders of Izapa anticipated the future to a degree that had us in mind and that they left us a star map encoded in a drawing of a mythological tale; we're just not convinced that they did.

Another theory, this one with completely imaginary links to the Maya, blames the sun. As in the movie *2012*, the eruption of massive solar flares will send solar particles to earth. In the movie, the poles shifted, there was rapid continental drift, and the planet was swept with tidal waves thousands of feet high. The film did not take itself too seriously, but in his book *Apocalypse 2012*, Lawrence Joseph predicts earnestly that solar flares will reverse the Earth's magnetic field. The Indian Ocean tsunamis of 2004, and Hurricane Katrina the following year—so the theory goes—all anticipated the natural disasters that we must expect in 2012. The supposed link between Maya wisdom and the threat of the sun is bandied about wildly, especially on Internet sites. But one searches in vain for even the slimmest possible evidence that the Maya predicted a solar event in 2012; there is not even a misinterpretation to be exploded.

~

We have focused in this chapter on the supposed evidence for 2012 and end-of-world predictions by the pre-Columbian Maya—that is, in sources dating from before the arrival of Europeans in Maya lands in the early sixteenth century. But, as outlined in the previous chapter, there were Maya texts written alphabetically in the centuries after the European invasion, texts that have been interpreted as clearly articulating Maya concepts of apocalypse.

Our contention is that such sources cannot be viewed in the same category as pre-Columbian sources; they cannot be seen as simply "Maya," untainted by European cultures and ideas. The books and websites on 2012 are riddled with a careless treatment of historical periods and geographical regions. But muddling up units of time and space destroys the potential for ancient and historical sources to tell us about the past; it prevents the Maya from communicating to us what they really thought.

To highlight the importance of the discrete nature of historical periods and cultural developments in particular regions, we now step away from the Maya—in fact, away from the Americas completely. To understand if and how Europeans altered Maya views of their past and our future, we need to know what kinds of ideas Spaniards brought across the Atlantic Ocean in the sixteenth century. The next chapter therefore focuses on medieval Europe. We then return to Mesoamerica, accompanying the Spanish friars first to central Mexico (chapter 4) and then back into Maya country (chapter 5).

· 3 ·

God Is Angry

The Millenarian Mother Lode

"I tell you that the Church of God must be renewed, and soon, for God is angry."

—Girolamo Savonarola, apocalyptic
Florentine preacher, 1490s

"And we know that we are bound above all to observe all these things by the commandments of the Lord and the constitutions of holy Mother Church. And let him who does not act thus know that he shall have to render an account therefore before our Lord Jesus Christ on the day of judgment."

—attributed to St. Francis of Assisi, thirteenth century

*F*ame and fortune came to the German artist at the tender age of twenty-seven. Albrecht Dürer had engraved a set of fifteen images, accompanied by text from the Bible. Innovatively, the text acted more as captions to the images rather than the engravings illustrating the text. Published simultaneously in Latin and German, the engravings were an instant success. And a lasting one—they have permanently changed the way in which we see and understand the biblical passages from which they draw (or, which they draw).

What were these images? They were first published in 1498, at a time when word of the discovery of a New World across the ocean was circulating in Europe. Did they depict the Garden of Eden, which Columbus thought he had discovered on the coasts of South America? Or did they illustrate conversion and salvation (the New World was populated by peoples who knew nothing of Christianity)? In fact, Dürer selected the Book of Revelation, and his series of engravings was titled *Apocalypse with Pictures*. Europeans loved the German artist's chosen topic—the cataclysmic end of the world—and the pear-wood blocks remained a lucrative source of income for Dürer for the rest of his life.

The most famous of the woodcuts is *The Four Horsemen of the Apocalypse*—it soon became Western civilization's most universal and enduring end-of-world image. But the series also included a number of scenes featuring St. John, various angels, *The Whore of Babylon*, and three different renderings of reptilian monsters: *St. Michael Fighting the Dragon*; *The Sea Monster and the Beast with the Lamb's Horn*; and *The Apocalyptic Woman* (figure 13). These monsters remind one of the great caiman of Maya mythology, vomiting out the Flood in the Dresden Codex, or needing to be slain for the world to be created anew in the *Books of Chilam Balam*. We are not suggesting a causal connection or odd coincidence—fear of reptiles, especially ones made large and monstrous, is common to human cultures throughout history—but merely noting the interesting parallel. On the other hand, the *Books of Chilam Balam* were written after Dürer's drawings were published (the possible implications of which we shall address in chapter 5).

So how do we explain the success of Dürer's woodcuts? The primal fear of reptilian monsters is not enough, neither would it suffice to investigate the artist's personal religious interests. The explanation lies in the larger culture that provided such fertile ground for the reception of the engravings.

Medieval Europe was in fact a hotbed of apocalyptic imaginings. Fears of the world's end, and hopes that a savior will come to replace the flawed world with a better one, developed not only in Mesoamer-

13. Albrecht Dürer, *The Apocalyptic Woman*, 1498.

ica and the Mediterranean but also in many times and places in history. But nowhere can match the latter for the depth and frequency of such hopes and fears. In short, Western civilization is the millenarian mother lode.

But, like all cultural developments, European millennialism of the medieval period did not develop in an intellectual vacuum. The theology illustrated by Dürer and debated by innumerable Christian clerics has its root in the older monotheistic religion from which Christianity emerged, Judaism.

～

Daniel must have been nervous as he was brought before Nebuchadnezzar, King of Babylon. Years earlier, in 606 BC, Babylonian invaders had taken Daniel from his home in Jerusalem. Perceiving him to be a smart young boy, his captors had him trained as a court advisor. In time, Daniel developed a reputation as a gifted interpreter of dreams and visions. As the king had been plagued for months by a series of disturbing nightmares, he therefore had Daniel summoned. Despite their best efforts, no one in Nebuchadnezzar's court could determine what the royal nightmares meant. The king had promised that the wise men "will receive from me gifts and rewards and great honor" if they could explain the dreams. But if they continued to fail him, "I will have you cut into pieces and your houses turned into piles of rubble."

Eventually, driven mad with frustration, Nebuchadnezzar ordered the execution of all of the kingdom's wise men. At that point, Daniel stepped forward to try his hand. Praying to God, he had a vision in which God explained the dream's ultimate meaning. The resulting description and interpretation of Nebuchadnezzar's dream, preserved in the Old Testament, is one of history's earliest written records of millennial belief.

Daniel vividly described how the king dreamt of a large statue, composed of various types of materials—the head "made of pure gold, its chest and arms of silver, its belly and thighs of bronze, its legs of iron, its feet partly of iron and partly of baked clay." In the dream, Nebuchadnezzar saw a rock, cut out "not by human hands," fall upon the statue, violently dismantling it. Once the statue had been obliterated, a strong wind swept away the debris and the rock grew into a "huge mountain that filled the whole earth." Daniel explained that the different parts of the statue represent a succession of different earthly kingdoms of varying quality. Babylonia was represented by the statue's golden head; Nebuchadnezzar was, after all, the "king of kings." Following the inevitable destruction of Babylonia, interpreted Daniel, another will rise up, of a slightly lesser quality—as symbolized by the statue's silver chest and arms. But the divine rock will also bring this rule to an end. Accordingly, two other even less qualified rulers will come to power, the bronze belly and thighs, followed by the divided kingdom composed of iron and clay, the statue's legs and feet. In the course of this human history, God will be setting "up a kingdom that will never be destroyed," the divinely quarried rock that served to destroy all of the earthly kingdoms.

Daniel not only interpreted the Babylonian king's nightmare but also himself had many dreams that foretold the destruction of earthly kingdoms and the subsequent creation of a divinely led earth. Daniel was not the first person to dream up such ideas; apocalyptic concepts of earthly destruction and recreation are found in other religious literatures in the Mediterranean and Near East in the centuries before the Christian era. But the story of Daniel and Nebuchadnezzar perfectly introduces the theme of millenarianism in Judaeo-Christian civilization for three reasons: first, for its antiquity and lasting popularity; second, because it shows how the notion of cycles of creation was by no means unique to the civilizations developing in Mesoamerica at this time; and third, because it illustrates the relevance of Jewish eschatology to the Christian millenarian tradition that developed in Europe during the Middle Ages.

According to the Tanakh, the Hebrew Bible, human history will last a mere 6,000 years. These six millennia are divided into three periods of 2,000 years each. The first period was one of *tohu* ("void" or "chaos"); the second 2,000 year period began with the life of Abraham; the third era is that of the messiah, who will come at the start (or during) that final period. Jewish eschatology—a branch of theology that studies the end of the world—concerns the appearance of this messiah, who will usher in a new era of human history.

Unlike Christianity, which deems Jesus Christ as a living incarnate of God and thus a divine being, those of the Jewish faith believe that their messiah will not be divine. Instead, the Jewish messiah will be completely human, born of two parents (and thus not of an immaculate conception) and be a descendent of King David. Nonetheless, this human messiah will be capable of uniting humankind; this two-thousand-year Messianic Era will thus be a time of global peace. The birth and revelation of the Jewish messiah terminates the older phase of human history; it will mark the end of the world as we have known it. The signs that the Messianic Era is at hand include the gathering of the Jewish faithful at the Holy Land, a defeat of Israel's enemies, the construction of the third temple in Jerusalem, and the resurrection of the dead. Some sources assert that Gog, king of Magog, will attack Israel, but God will intervene and save the Jewish people. This is the world's final defeat of good over evil. Over the centuries Gog and Magog have been variously identified—as the Mongol hoards, for example, or as Russia, or more recently as Saddam Hussein and Iraq.

There have been many false alarms and many claimants to the messianic mantle, but no candidate more successful—thus far, and in some senses—than Jesus Christ. Evolving out of Judaism, early Christianity appropriated and repackaged many older traditions and ideas. Among others, Daniel was brought along for the ride; Jesus himself is quoted as referencing the "end of age" prediction of "Daniel the prophet" when he warns his apostles that after his death God will again return to earth. In fact, during the first few centuries of Christianity, it was commonly believed that Christ himself would return to earth for a thousand years. Hippolytus of Rome (c. 176–235) argued that it would be six thousand years before the Second Coming. The idea—called premillenialism—that Christ would return in the flesh and remain on earth for those years was declared heresy in the fourth century.

But it persisted, and related ideas flourished as well. In second-century Turkey, the imminent return of Christ was preached by Montanus; although his predictions proved disappointing and the cult was eventually declared heretical by the Church, Montanism spread to various regions of the Roman Empire and lasted for centuries.

Even in its barest bones, the Montanist story contains two key elements that have remained central to millenarianism—up to and including the 2012 phenomenon. These are, first, the repeated declaration that the end is nigh, often with a specific given date that inevitably proves to be an anticlimax; failure is explained in terms of miscalculations, the difficulty we have as sinners to understand God's will, or various other excuses leading to the declaration of a new date. Second, the notion that the Apocalypse is imminent inevitably finds fertile ground among the dispossessed, those with the least to lose in the conflagration of Doomsday; the established powers of church and state are more likely to feel threatened. Since Montanus, urgent apocalyptic preaching has tended toward the revolutionary and has been muzzled as a result. Indeed, suppression is part of what gives such ideas their credibility; hence the insistence by some 2012ologists writing outside of academia that university professors have been trying to shut them up with denial and derision.

In parallel to the spread of cults such as the Montanists, for the half-millennium leading up to the sixth century, a network of sects across Europe known to us as the Gnostics pursued and promoted the notion that "true knowledge" was the path to salvation. Gnosticism holds that Christians should not simply surrender to faith and accept that most things can only be known by God; instead, they should examine all sources of knowledge, including those of other religions and cultures, in order to uncover the truth. There is a hidden wisdom in the text—or, more likely, in the numbers—waiting to be discovered by the capable and dedicated.

Faced with opposition and eventually violent repression from the Church, Gnosticism increasingly became a movement of covert sages, sacred codes, and tales of ancient wisdom suppressed by corrupt earthly powers. If this sounds like a familiar story, it is probably because you have read or seen the *Da Vinci Code* books, movies, and related literature; but it may also be because the spirit of Gnosticism is very much alive in the 2012 phenomenon (a thread we pick up in chapter 6).

The eschatology that helped define Christianity, particularly that of the medieval period, was partly derived from the Book of Daniel, partly based on the mystical interpretations of events described in the Book of the Revelation of John. Although through the centuries clerics and scholars have used the same biblical passages to divergent ends, most understand this section of the New Testament as a vivid, predictive description. It is widely believed within Christian theology to describe what is going to happen at the end of the world, a foreseeing of the world after the destruction of its current form.

The Book of Revelation's depiction of the terrifying events that will come to pass served as fodder not only for graphic artists such as Dürer (see figures 13, 14, and 17) but also whetted the imaginations of medieval period mystics. These closing New Testament passages describe how God's message will be given to John via an angel. John has a set of visions, specifically seven messages to seven different churches, all clothed in a cosmic battle between good and evil. After a series of catastrophic events, deserving people are saved by a "Lamb" who destroys the evil in the world by throwing Satan in a pit for one thousand years. This new millennium of peace is often called the "Second Coming of Christ," after a reference in John 14:3 to Jesus' life on earth as his "first coming."

After these thousand years, Satan will be released, some suggest for a seven-year period called the Tribulation. A massive war between the forces of good and evil will ensue—the oft-cited Armageddon, from which Dürer culled his print series. While most human beings will be killed in this struggle, eventually Satan will be defeated. The remaining people who are not true Christians will be sent to Hades during the Last Judgment, another favorite subject of early modern artists (see figure 14; Dürer again). Christ will then descend to earth again, during his Rapture. This new era is defined by a unification of the people with God and the linking of the spiritual and the earthly, resulting in a heavenly city called the "New Jerusalem."

Over the centuries, numerous theologians interpreted these biblical passages as apocalyptic foretelling, thereby ensuring that apocalyptic thought would have a lasting effect on late medieval and then

14. Albrecht Dürer, *The Last Judgment*, 1510.

early modern philosophy. Indeed, interpretations and images of the Last Judgment are commonplace in medieval literature, art, and on public sculpture. One example—which we have chosen for its artistic merit and because it evokes again that universal theme of the fear of reptilian monsters—is the tiny painting of *The Last Judgment* from the psalter of Henry of Bloise (figure 15).

Henry may have used this beautiful prayer book, with its eighty miniature illustrations, on a daily basis. In the psalter's depiction of Judgment Day, the jaws of two beasts form Hellmouth, an apocalyptic image that originated in ninth-century England and remained popular in religious art—and even in theater, as a scary prop device—into the sixteenth century (and we shall see it in Mexico in the next chapter). The appearance inside hell of kings and queens, naked save for their crowns, being torn apart by demons along with others was central to the potentially radical nature of apocalyptic thinking. One can only imagine that Henry hoped that the final day would not come in his lifetime; he was brother to the English king and Bishop of Winchester from 1129 until his death in 1171.

15. *The Hellmouth*, twelfth century.

Probably the best-known promoter of millennial thinking in writing was Joachim of Fiore, a late twelfth-century theologian born on the island of Sicily. After making a pilgrimage to the Holy Land at a young age, Joachim returned to the Italian Peninsula and wandered as a hermit before eventually becoming a priest and an abbot under the Cistercian order. The focal point of Joachim's academic work was the interpretation of the Book of Revelation, which he understood as describing an ordered account for all of human history; that he was remembered for his writings on the Apocalypse is reflected in this fifteenth-century woodcut portrait of him (figure 16).

Joachim of Fiore divided time into three stages, clearly referencing the symbolism of the Christian trinity, what he called the "Eternal Gospel." The first age was named "The Age of the Father" and was linked to the time period and events recalled in the Old Testament. Joachim described this first age as an era when humans obediently lived in accord with the rules of God the father. The following human age, "The Age of the Son," began with the birth of Christ. Based on Joachim's interpretation of passages in Revelation mentioning events lasting 1,260 days, he predicted that this second human age would end in AD 1260, commencing his third age, "The Age of the Holy Spirit." This final human era would be defined as a time when humans would be in direct contact with God and finally capable of fully understanding his words. This era would be marked by peace, the creation of an idyllic earthly realm where the authority of the Catholic Church would not be needed.

Joachim's work was both accepted and then condemned during his lifetime, as well as in subsequent years—particularly after 1260 passed without the apocalypse and the much-hoped-for human union with the Christian godhead (inevitably perhaps, anticlimax and disappointment have become integral to the Western millenarian tradition). But the trying times of late-medieval Europe—plague, famine, war—were fertile ground for apocalyptic visionaries. One of the most effective, colorful, and—let's face it—unlikeable was Girolamo Savonarola (1452–1498).

16. *Woodcut Portrait of Joachim of Fiore*, 1612.

A northern Italian scholar and Dominican friar from a privileged background, Savonarola discovered a talent for what might be called performance preaching. In the Florence of the 1490s he became an increasingly radical and hysterical public figure, ranting against wealth, power, corruption, whorishness, and homosexuality. Christian thought was corrupted by an evil kowtowing to classical scholars; reason itself was an instrument of the devil. The works of Plato and Aristotle, and all those who studied them, should be burned, along with all poetry, one of art's "lowest forms." Savonarola channeled Christianity's millenarian tradition into a series of dramatic, revolutionary sermons, pamphlets, books, and engravings depicting the end of the comfy and wicked world that Florentines took for granted. He spoke of having visions in which "swords, knives, lances, and every weapon" rained down on the people of the city—or the whole peninsula: "I saw a sword, which quivered over Italy, turn its point downward and, with the greatest storm and scourge, go among them and flay them all."

The friar urged the people to repent their sins immediately, as the end was at hand and "later there will be no room for penitence." Savonarola did not bother offering specific dates for when the Last Judgment would occur; there was no time left for that. He was not the first to claim that the end of the world was already upon us, and— more importantly—he was not the last. His insistence that the end of the world could be divined not by calculations and learning but by opening one's eyes to the preapocalyptic lifestyles of the world around was a notion that has resonated through the centuries since his death (burned at the stake in 1498). Arguably, the quasiscientific arguments for taking 2012 seriously—the details of Maya calendrics, the analysis of planetary movements—would not have flourished in recent years without the fertile ground of modern millenarianism. And as much as Savonarola was in many ways a medieval figure, he also anticipated the anxiety in the modern West over how and why the world is going to hell in a handbasket. As historian Felipe Fernández-Armesto has put it, Savonarola's

> addiction to millenarianism, his confidence in visions, his prophetic stridency, his hatred of art, and his mistrust of secular scholarship align him with aspects of the modern world most

moderns reject: religious obscurantism, extreme fanaticism, irrational fundamentalism. In some ways, the conflicts he brought to a head—the confrontation of worldly and godly moralities, the uncomprehending debate between rational and subrational or suprarational mind-sets, the struggle for power in the state between the partisans of secularism and spirituality or of science and scripture—are timeless, universal features of history. Yet they are also, in their current intensity and ferocity, among the latest novelties of contemporary politics. The culture wars of our own time did not begin with Savonarola, but he embodied some of their most fearsome features.

~

In 1503 Dürer was at it again (or rather, still at it, given his impressive lifetime production). This time, rather than create a series of prints illustrating apocalyptic events, the German artist created multiple engravings detailing the lives of the Saints; the success of the engravings helped to popularize in the collective imagination the miracles that gained each saint their renown.

In *St. Francis Receiving the Stigmata*, Dürer depicted the pivotal moment in the life of St. Francis, the miracle that essentially earned him his sanctity (figure 17). According to legend derived from an eye-witness account, St. Francis had retreated to Mount Verna (located in the Tuscan region of Italy) in 1224 to fast for forty days. This was intended as a form of corporeal penance but also as an attempt to replicate the self-sacrifice of Christ and his apostles. Suddenly, St. Francis had a "vision of a seraph, a six-winged angel," vividly imaged in the upper left side of the composition, visually prominent as the form is set against the white emptiness of background clouds. This is no ordinary angel but instead is a kind of winged crucifix, an image of Christ on the cross aloft with six appended wings. The angel forcefully emits five beams of light that reach down from the heavens and are intercepted by the body of St. Francis himself. The beams conveniently hit five meaningful points within the context of Christian lore, the palms of the Saint's hands, the tops of his feet, and the lower right side

17. Albrecht Dürer, *St. Francis Receiving the Stigmata*, 1503–1504.

of his torso, the five places wounded on the body of Christ during his crucifixion. In Dürer's rendition, this violence causes Francis to throw his head back, presumably in pain, but also to look upward toward his assailant.

Despite St. Francis's obvious discomfort, the only person to witness the miracle, Brother Leo—shown in the image's middle ground, warily watching the event out of the corner of his eye—recounted that "this angel gave him the gift of the five wounds of Christ." In phrasing the wounds as a "gift," Brother Leo summarizes the entire purpose and intention of the religious order founded by St. Francis: the emulation of the life of Christ and his apostles. A few centuries later, the Franciscans would spearhead the Christian campaign against Aztec and Maya cultures. Of all the religious orders that ended up in the Americas, the Franciscans maintained the most profound and well-articulated millennial ideology, and their order was the branch of the Church that most heavily influenced the later millennial traditions of the New World (as we shall see in the two chapters to follow). A short foray into the order's origin and core beliefs is thus necessary.

Legends surround both the early life and later religious experiences of St. Francis of Assisi (1182–1226), but we will summarize the main points here. Born in Italy to a wealthy merchant family, Giovanni Francesco di Bernadone showed signs of disillusion with the material world at an early age. Rather than follow in his father Pietro's footsteps and amass wealth via international trade, a series of ecstatic visions prompted Francesco to dedicate his life to the poor. In his twenties he did various acts of charity, such as tending to lepers and begging for alms in the name of poverty. According to his life accounts, hearing one sermon in particular changed the course of the young Francesco's life. The priest spoke of how Jesus had told the apostles to live as paupers, to "heal the sick, raise the dead, cleanse those who have leprosy, drive out demons" and to preach that "the kingdom of heaven is near."

After this sermon, Francis decided to fully emulate the apostles, dedicating himself to a life of poverty and proselytizing on the imminence of the "the kingdom of heaven." Donning a simple woolen robe, and without shoes, money, or other means, Francis began preaching. Others followed suit, and in 1209 Pope Innocent III granted Francis and his group of eleven like-minded individuals permission to start a new religious order. They would be known as the "Order of the Friars Minor." They followed a truly ascetic lifestyle, defined by abstinence from most worldly pleasure—including, but certainly not limited to, food, sex, and physical comforts. As stated later in the order's rule of 1223:

> The brothers should appropriate neither house, nor place, nor anything for themselves; and they should go confidently after alms, serving God in poverty and humility, as pilgrims and strangers in this world. Nor should they feel ashamed, for God made Himself poor in this world for us. This is that peak of

the highest poverty which has made you, my dearest brothers, heirs and kings of the kingdom of heaven, poor in things but rich in virtues.

The purpose of the rule was to bring the order's members in closer communion with God so as to better prepare themselves—and those to whom they preached—for the Second Coming, as referenced in the introductory quote. The Franciscans were, in other words, mystics, believers in the power of prayer and lifestyle to achieve direct contact with God. Medieval Franciscan mysticism's two apexes were, in the words of a venerable historian of the order, "the image of the Apocalypse and the sanctification of poverty." From the thirteenth to sixteenth centuries, the Franciscans appropriated, developed, and in many ways embodied the millennium-old Western tradition of Messianic and prophetic mysticism.

This tradition did not end in the sixteenth century—in fact, it was stimulated by the rise of Protestantism, invigorated by the rise of capitalism and the scientific revolution, and survives in multiple forms today, not least of which is the 2012 phenomenon. But what is just as significant to the thread of our argument here, perhaps more so, is the fact that the final great flowering of medieval apocalyptical mysticism and missionizing took place in the Americas. Who led the spiritual assault upon pagan faith in the Americas? The Franciscans. When the first Europeans reached major civilizations in the Americas, whom did they contact? The peoples of Mesoamerica—the Aztecs and other speakers of Nahuatl, the Mixtecs and Zapotecs, and the Maya.

～

There is a vast literature on millenarianism in Europe and the Mediterranean in the thousands of years leading up to the discovery of the New World; what we have offered here is a potted history designed to hammer down one simple point. Whereas millenarianism is not easily and clearly found in ancient Maya civilization, it is deeply rooted and ubiquitous in Western civilization. Whereas Maya notions of world-ending Apocalypse are muted and obscure, the Apocalypse—with a capital A—was a profound and pervasive presence in the medieval West. The contrast could not be starker. We are told that the Maya predicted the world's end in 2012. Yet, as we saw in the previous chapter, Maya culture is a Doomsday dead end; it is the West that is the millenarian mother lode.

Furthermore, apocalyptic anxieties mounted in Europe in the decades leading up to the Spanish invasion of the Americas. The European discovery of the New World served only to encourage such concerns, while the arm of the Church that led the spiritual assault upon the Aztecs, Mayas, and their neighbors was one of the orders most deeply imbued in apocalyptic ideology. It is that story—the impact of the Franciscans upon native cultures, and, ultimately, 2012ology—to which we now turn.

· 4 ·

The Moctezuma Factor

The End of the World Comes to Mexico

"The Most High was pleased to display before us a continent, new lands, and an unknown world."

—Amerigo Vespucci, 1504

"The Middle Ages sang its swan song in the New World in the sixteenth century."

—John Phelan, *The Millennial Kingdom of the Franciscans in the New World*, 1956

"For a time I have been concerned, looking toward the mysterious place from which you have come, among clouds and mist . . . and now it has come true, you have come. Be doubly welcomed, enter the land, go to enjoy your palace; rest your body. May our lords be arrived in the land!"

—Moctezuma, emperor of the Aztecs, to Hernando Cortés, 1519

*T*he Aztec Empire was defeated not by Spanish invaders but by the millenarian beliefs of the emperor, Moctezuma. The great Mexican empire was rapidly destroyed not by Cortés the conquistador but by Quetzalcoatl, an Aztec god. This, at least, was the story told both by

Spaniards and Aztecs in the sixteenth century, and it has persisted at the heart of narratives of the Conquest of Mexico to this day.

The kernel of this interpretation of the Conquest is the tale of an ancient king who ruled the Mexican kingdom of Tula centuries before the rise of the Aztecs (or, more properly, the Mexica). Named Quetzalcoatl (Feathered Serpent), he fell from power and went into exile. But rather than dying, he became divine and was destined to return. A Feathered Serpent deity had been worshiped in Mesoamerica for centuries, perhaps millennia; the Maya called him Kukulcan or Kucumatz (which likewise means "feathered serpent" in Yucatec and Quiché Mayan). So the legend of the exiled ruler merged with the mythology of Quetzalcoatl, god of wind and knowledge (figure 18 is one rendering of the god in a sixteenth-century codex).

Hernando Cortés told the Spanish king, in a letter written in 1520 (in the middle of his two-year war of invasion against the Aztecs), that Moctezuma himself told him a version of this tale. The people of Mexico had always believed, said the emperor, that the descendents of this ancient ruler "would come and subjugate this land and take us as their vassals." Moctezuma continued to Cortés:

> So according to the place from which you say you come, which is where the sun rises, and the things you tell us of the great lord or king who sent you here, we believe and we are certain that he must be our natural lord, especially because you say that he has known of us for a long time. So be assured that we will obey you and will hold you as lord in place of that great lord of which you tell us.

Cortés not surprisingly made much of the idea that Moctezuma greeted him either as a *returning* lord or as the representative of the ruler for whom the Aztecs had been waiting. It enlisted the supposedly superstitious beliefs of the Aztecs to give credence to the otherwise improbable claim that the emperor had not only welcomed Cortés but also immediately surrendered to him. The letter quoted

18. Quetzalcoatl, from the Codex Telleriano-Remensis, sixteenth century.

above was available in print in Spain as early as 1522, so the story of the emperor's speech of surrender rapidly became common currency in narratives of the Conquest.

It has remained so up to the present, with Conquest-era judgments on Moctezuma reverberating loudly in modern histories. For example, the famous juxtaposition written in 1543 by Juan Ginés de Sepúlveda of "a noble, valiant Cortés with a timorous, cowardly Moctezuma" is echoed in Barbara Tuchman's classic 1984 study of the failure of leadership from the Trojan Horse to the disaster of Vietnam. The Aztec emperor, she wrote, was a "fatal and tragic example" of the folly and "mental standstill" that can paralyze a ruler:

> Through an excess of mysticism or superstition, he had apparently convinced himself that the Spaniards were indeed the party of Quetzalcoatl come to register the break-up of his empire and, believing himself doomed, made no effort to avert his fate.

Put another way, in a line read and no doubt swallowed as neat fact by tens of thousands of readers of Jared Diamond's Pulitzer Prize–winning *Guns, Germs, and Steel*: "Montezuma miscalculated even more grossly when he took Cortés for a returning god."

Do we only have the victors' version of the Spanish invasion, the West's view of events running consistently from Cortés to Diamond? In fact, there are also some accounts written down in the sixteenth century in Nahuatl (the language of the central Mexicans, Aztecs included), giving us potential insight into the Aztec perspective. The best known of these, a passage from an epic work later dubbed the Florentine Codex, reproduces Moctezuma's speech of welcome. *Totecuioe oticmihiovilti, oticmociavilti, otlaltitech tommaxitico*, began the emperor, "Oh our lord, be doubly welcomed on your arrival in this land!" Standing tall before the conquistador, face to face, Moctezuma went on:

> You have come to satisfy your curiosity about your city-state of Mexico, you have come to sit on your seat of authority, which I have kept a while for you, where I have been in charge for you, for your agents the rulers who have gone, who for a very short time came to be in charge for you.

Naming the five emperors who ruled the Aztec domain before him, Moctezuma depicts Cortés himself as the legitimate lord of the empire; the preceding century of emperors have merely been regents, keeping the throne warm for its true holder.

The story of Moctezuma's supposed superstition-inspired surrender of the Aztec Empire to a few hundred Spaniards is not the red herring to our tale that it might seem to be. The terms used by Tuchman, for example—doom, fate, mysticism—are the language of millenarianism. The conventional narrative has Moctezuma undone by belief in the power of prediction. There is even an astronomical component to the story; Moctezuma's pre-Conquest nerves are undone by a series of bad omens, the first of which is a comet, "a flaming ear of corn" seen in the sky (see figure 23 at this chapter's end). The implication is that the Aztecs had developed millenarian beliefs and expectations, that these were deeply rooted in central Mexican cultures, and that they were so important as to potentially influence major events—such as the collapse of the greatest empire the region had seen. Either this was true (and we search for 2012 roots in central Mexico) or it was not (and we search for the roots of the Moctezuma millenarian myth).

~

As the sun set on the volcanoes and lakeside towns of the Basin of Mexico, a procession of Aztec priests left the great plaza at the heart of the Aztec capital. With the towering temple-pyramids of Tenochtitlán's ceremonial center at their backs, they walked across the causeway that linked the island-city to the eastern banks of Lake Texcoco. There they climbed the gentle slope of the small mountain of Huixachtlán, to the temple at its summit, where they could be seen from almost anywhere in the Basin.

The Aztec Empire was dark; all fires had been extinguished, in preparation for the ritual then unfolding. As midnight approached, the Basin's hundreds of thousands of inhabitants climbed on walls, rooftops, hills, anywhere that gave them a view of Huixachtlán. As Orion's Belt—the Fire Drill constellation—became visible in the evening sky, priests removed the heart of a sacrificial victim and placed a

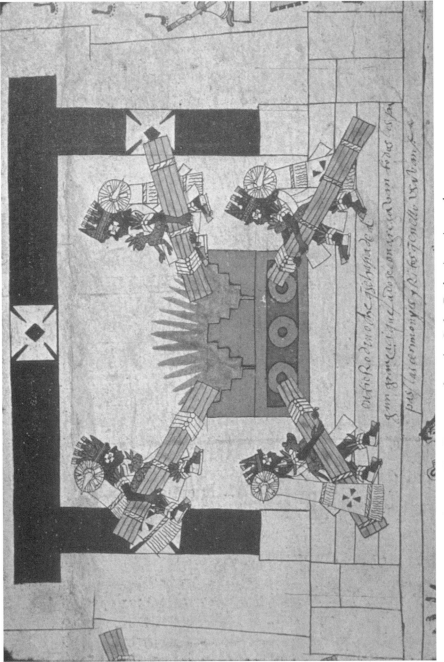

19. The New Fire Ceremony, from the Codex Borbonicus, sixteenth century.

fire drill in his chest cavity. The victim was chosen through a careful selection process; his name had to contain the term *Xiuitl*, which means both "fire" and "year" in Nahuatl. In this Xiuitl's chest, sparks were made, then a small flame, then the first fire of the new fifty-two-year calendar round. Light returned to the empire. Soon, a great bonfire was created, into which bundles of sticks were thrust, turned into torches, and taken down into the city to light fires in the temples (see figure 19). They began with the two great temples to the deities of war and rain, then took the flame to lesser temples, to private homes in the city, and finally out to the temples, towns, and villages of the empire.

This ritual—known to us as the New Fire Ceremony—took place in Mexico in some form or another every fifty-two years for at least a millennium. The one described above, the only one for which we have written and visual evidence (such as the Codex Borbonicus, excerpted in figure 19), was the last New Fire Ceremony ever enacted. It was held in 1507, five years after Moctezuma became emperor. It symbolizes two important perspectives on Aztec history—two points that allow us to dismantle and correct the impression given by the narrative that began this chapter.

The first point is about how the Aztecs viewed the turn of the calendrical cycle. Did the Aztecs fear that without the New Fire Ceremony to initiate the next fifty-two years, their world would end? Most likely not. There is no doubt that such rituals were taken seriously by the Aztecs and other Mesoamericans, that they were seen as vital and efficacious. But there is little sign that Mesoamericans anticipated the end of the next cycle with great anxiety or with the expectation that it would impact them and their families. In other words, rituals like the New Fire Ceremony were celebrations of renewal and rebirth, not manifestations of millenarian concern.

For the Aztecs, this lack of concern can be largely explained by the vagueness of the larger cycle. For one thing, the Aztecs had no equivalent to the Maya Long Count. There is no evidence that a long count was ever recorded in central Mexico, and even the Maya one

had fallen into disuse half a millennium before the rise of the Aztec
Empire. Furthermore, whereas the Maya believed they lived in the
fourth creation of the world, the Aztecs believed the present one was
the fifth. Not only that, but the previous creations were of varying
lengths. The first was 676 years (thirteen cycles of fifty-two years),
the second 364 (seven cycles of fifty-two), the third 312 years (six
cycles), and the fourth back to 676 years. So how long was the fifth
cycle to be? The Aztecs believed that earthquakes would mark the
sixth creation of the world, but there was no apparent consensus or
common belief as to how long the fifth cycle would be.

Aztec notions of these great cosmic cycles are illustrated on the
Calendar Stone, perhaps the most easily recognized art object created
in the indigenous Americas (figure 20). This monumental sculpture
measures twelve feet across, is four feet thick, and weighs more than

20. The Calendar Stone, 1479.

twenty-four tons. It likely functioned as a small platform, viewed from above. Iconographically complex, the sculpture was originally brightly painted. Composed of a series of concentric rings, the central ring hosts the outward-looking face of the Aztec sun or earth deity (scholars debate which one), whose outstretched fists hold human hearts.

Surrounding this god, four dates are illustrated, each of which commemorate the day on which the previous four eras ended cataclysmically. The first era, represented in the square cartouche in the upper right, is symbolically referred to by the date of 4 Jaguar, recalling when the era's inhabitants, immense giants, were violently destroyed by fierce wild cats. The world was created anew but then succumbed on the date 4 Wind due to hurricanes, as seen in the upper left square cartouche. The era 4 Rain followed (represented in the lower left square cartouche), when a horrific rain of fire consumed the world. The fourth era, 4 Water, as seen in the lower right cartouche, came to an end after a flood had destroyed life on earth. This brings us to the fifth era, one that will supposedly end on the date 4 Earthquake; the Doomsday event will be—you guessed it—a massive geological tremor.

It is easy to see how this monument has been used, more than any other Aztec text, sculpture, or art, to illustrate the supposed millenarianism of the Aztecs. It does refer to the Aztec idea of previous eras of creation, each of which was destroyed rather violently. But nowhere on the monument (nor anywhere in any form or expression of Aztec culture) is there evidence that the world would not begin anew.

In fact, the very ideology of time as a series of cycles marked inevitably by renewal is represented elsewhere in the monument itself. In addition to the four dates described above, two other dates are carved on the monument. The date 1 Flint Knife, located near the middle of the image, had both cosmological and political importance to the sculpture's Aztec audience: it referenced the time when the Aztecs began their migration from their mythological place of origin, Lake Aztlan and was also the date (in 1428) when they defeated a rival Basin of Mexico population (the Tepanecs), allowing the Aztecs to ascend to power. The other additional calendrical date, 13 Reed, refers both to the creation date of the current world and to the moment when the first Aztec emperor, Itzcoatl, ascended to the throne by defeating another rival city-state in the Basin, Azcapotzalco.

The purpose of these pairings is transparently political and decidedly not apocalyptic; Aztec imperial ideology was well developed, sophisticated, and "sold" to the empire's subjects in multiple complex packages, the Calendar Stone being just one example. The references to 1 Flint Knife and 13 Reed linked mythical events from the deep past, or "mythistory," to military and political triumphs achieved recently and locally by the Aztecs; the empire's rulers thereby claimed that Aztec hegemony was as much a fact of life—and just as legitimate—as the world itself. The message was: Aztec rule is an integral facet of the current world, as it should be; this world is not about to end; on the contrary, it and its rulers are here to stay, to see out the cycle and—think of the New Fire Ceremony—not only survive but also manage the transition to the next cycle.

One final point about the misuse of the Calendar Stone: it has been appropriated to illustrate calendar-based millenarianism not only among the Aztecs but also among the Maya. The stone adorns 2012 books, novels, websites, and a multitude of other graphic formats. We have already seen two such examples—figure 11, based on an online newspaper graphic, and the Bizarro cartoon in figure 1; the fact that the Calendar Stone's misuse in the cartoon is irrelevant (the joke still works) reflects how common the misappropriation of the image has become. But, of course, the Calendar Stone has no bearing on anything Maya. Aztec and Maya cultures are both part of Mesoamerican civilization, but they are separate and distinct from each other. The Calendar Stone was carved in the Basin of Mexico (possibly in 1479, but probably during Moctezuma's reign of 1502–1520), many hundreds of miles and hundreds of years from anything even remotely related to the supposed Maya 2012 materials.

The second point to be made here, stemming from the New Fire Ceremony, is about Moctezuma himself. The Ceremony of 1507 was an example of how well the Aztecs appropriated old traditions for the religious and political purposes of their empire. By laying claim to the control of the calendar, they helped perpetuate their loose control over some sixty city-states across half a million square kilometers in central and southern Mexico—the entity we call the Aztec Empire. The 1507 ceremony also promoted the authority and legitimacy of Moctezuma as emperor. The later portrayal of him as ineffective, hesitant, even cowardly in the face of the Spanish invasion does not correlate with his record as ruler.

In fact, he was one of the empire's most dynamic and effective leaders, waging a series of successful campaigns to expand the empire south into what are now Oaxaca, Chiapas, and the Isthmus of Tehuantepec. Had it not been for the Spanish invasion, it would likely have been the captains of Moctezuma, not Cortés, who would have led Aztec warriors into Maya lands in the 1520s and 1530s; a 1559 New Fire Ceremony might have symbolized Aztec control over most of what is today Mexico and Guatemala. The Calendar Stone and the New Fire Ceremony not only illustrate Aztec imperial ideology but also specifically reflect Moctezuma's assertion of an awesome authority, one imbued with the powers of creation and cosmic-level control over the cycles of the calendar.

What therefore, of Moctezuma's surrender to Cortés without a fight, his speech of submission recorded in Spanish and Nahuatl sources alike? We have, as you will have anticipated, a different interpretation of the emperor and his meeting with the conquistador. But first, we must turn to the Franciscans and their arrival in the Americas.

~

It is somewhat mind-boggling to think that while the Aztecs were engaged in the New Fire Ceremony in 1507, a short distance to the east the Spaniards were a decade and a half into the exploration and settlement of the Caribbean; yet neither knew of each other's existence or the impact their mutual discovery would make on the world. Since Christopher Columbus had first returned to the Old World, in 1493, Europeans had wrestled with how to accommodate his findings to their worldview. The initial effect was less than dramatic: Columbus himself insisted he had found islands off the coast of East Asia, and the newness and extent of the discoveries were not widely promoted until the next decade, mostly by Amerigo Vespucci. For example, the Florentine voyager's *Mundus Novus* of 1504 popularized the term *New World* and anticipated how church scholars would interpret the discoveries. Take the description of one of Vespucci's Atlantic crossings, which allegedly took sixty-seven days, of which forty-four were:

> of constant rain, thunder and lightning—so dark that we never did see sun by day or fair sky by night. By reason of this, such fear invaded us that we soon abandoned all hope of life. But during these violent tempests of sea and sky, so numerous and so violent, the Most High was pleased to display before us a continent, new lands, and an unknown world. At sight of these things, we were filled with as much joy as anyone can imagine usually fall to the lot of those who have gained refuge from varied calamity and hostile fortune.

The tone of the piece is one of apocalypse and redemption. The ocean's watery grave and the totality of the tempest are a metaphor for the end of the world; the God-given New World is a metaphor for the idyllic millennium that follows. The voyagers are saved, and the new lands are the reason for their salvation.

The message was clear; Columbus had said it too: the New World was delivered to Christians for a purpose. Because the Bible makes no mention of the Americas, the use of the scriptures to make sense of their existence required some imagination. Not surprisingly—at least, according to our argument here—the discoveries across the Atlantic soon fed into Europe's long-standing fascination with the drama of the Apocalypse. This was largely thanks to a popular biblical exegesis circulating at the time. Nicholas de Lyra (1270–1349) was a French Franciscan and a professor at the Sorbonne in Paris; there he wrote the world's first commentary on the Bible. The commentary was not printed until 1471, but it was an instant and wild success, owned and repeatedly cited by historical figures such as Columbus and the influential Dominican friar Bartolomé de las Casas. For our tale, Lyra's interpretation of the Gospel of Luke is particularly pertinent, as it contains the biblical passage that would be most commonly used to justify the New World evangelical campaign.

In chapter 14 of Luke, Jesus, while a guest at the dinner table of "a prominent Pharisee," recounts a parable of a rather different dinner party. A stately lord was planning a banquet, and he called upon his servant to invite three guests to dine. One by one the guests declined, citing various excuses. The first had to look at a newly purchased field, the second had to try out a new head of oxen, and the third could not attend because he had recently been wed. Returning with these regrets, the servant was again dispatched by his master, but this time ordered to "Go out quickly into the streets and alleys of the town and bring in the poor, the crippled, the blind and the lame." The servant returned with these new guests, and when there was still room at the banquet table the lord ordered the servant to have it filled—so as to exclude the original guests, so that "not one of those men who were invited will get a taste of my banquet."

While this parable was told by Jesus as a means to teach a morality lesson on the importance of charity, in the millennial hotbed of medieval Europe it was transformed into a veiled reference to the world's impending doom. Under Lyra's pen, the lord became symbolic of Jesus Christ himself, dinnertime became the end of the world, and the banquet feast was the inevitable eternal bliss. And what of the other players in this parable? The servant came to represent the priests of the world, who call the masses to partake of the feast; the three guests who refused to partake were obviously references to the three pagan populations of the medieval world, the Jews, the Muslims, and the Gentiles.

The discovery of the Americas and its millions of indigenous inhabitants presented a massive, previously unknown population of Gentiles. As one of the principle prophesies of the Second Coming was the necessary conversion of all people on earth—and thus the creation of a truly universal Christianity—this seemingly impossible task was now deemed possible. The last unconverted population could now be accounted for. The time had come.

More so than the discovery of the islands in the 1490s, the realization in the 1520s that there was a vast, heavily settled mainland resounded loudly among the religious orders in Spain, especially the Franciscans. Symbolic of their response was the fact that the order sent a dozen friars—an Apostolic Twelve—into central Mexico in 1524. The head of the Franciscans in Spain instructed the Twelve to begin immediately the proselytization of its millions of Nahuas (Nahuatl-speakers) and other native peoples, "to convert by word and example" those who "are held captive with the blindness of idolatry under the yoke of Satan."

Ca yehuantin huel achtopa hualmohuicaque, "these were the very first who came," the native scribe of Puebla later wrote, listing their names and adding that "they brought here the holy things of our lord God." In nearby Tlaxcala, the entry in the town annals was the same: "Reed year. Here in this year the twelve friars came. They brought the holy things of our lord God . . . They were the ones who brought the faith, the Holy Gospel." The "things" were the sacraments; the new lord God had a name, written *Dioz* by Puebla's scribe; the new faith was the *Sancto Euagelio.* Tlaxcala had been an enemy of the Aztecs, resisting the empire for decades and then playing a central role in its destruction. But they did not replace the Aztecs; along with the Aztecs, who were fellow Nahuas (Nahuatl-speakers), the Tlaxcalans became subjects of New Spain, subjects of the new church. The new faith had come to replace the old one, as a later entry in the Tlaxcalan annals remarked, "5 Reed year. At this time the friars arrived. Then was the time that the devils' houses were demolished." The temples fell, the pyramids were decapitated, and in their place the new churches rose.

The conversion process—the Spiritual Conquest, as it became known—was not, of course, quite that simple. And, despite early claims of God-given successes on a vast scale, the Franciscans knew that the task was a challenge of epic proportions. The effect was to encourage the blossoming of millenarian justifications and expectations, especially as the decades passed and it became clear that this particular conquest was going to last generations. A "mystical interpretation of the conquest" emerged (in the words of one scholar), best exemplified by Gerónimo de Mendieta, a Franciscan whose take on the process was heavily influenced by Nicholas de Lyra's reading of Luke's gospel. Mendieta arrived from Spain in 1554 and dedicated his entire life to converting central Mexico's native peoples. His monumental account of the conversion campaign, titled *Historia eclesiástica indiana* (The History of the Church in the Indies), used the parable in Luke to explain the entire Spiritual Conquest.

Thanks to Lyra, the parable was already being read as a veiled reference to the Apocalypse and the Second Coming of Christ. Mendieta likewise saw the host as Jesus Christ and the meal as symbolizing "eternal happiness," with the mealtime as the end of the world. But while he accepted that the guests who refused to come to the banquet table represented the three unconverted populations of the early modern world—the Jews, the Muslims, and the Gentiles—Mendieta took his interpretation a step further. In his view, the three invitations are clues intended to refer to the different methods of conversion that friars should take when proselytizing to people of the three un-Christian faiths.

This highly pragmatic re-reading of the banquet parable gave practical advice on how to convert the remaining unconverted—all with the goal of bringing on the Second Coming. As Mendieta explained:

> By means of His illuminations, warnings and punishments, by means of His servants the patriarchs and prophets, by means of

His own son in person and later by means of the apostles, the martyrs, the preachers and the saints, God has been calling all the peoples of earth to hasten to prepare themselves to enter and to enjoy that everlasting feast that will be endless. This vocation of God shall not cease until the number of the predestined is reached, which according to the vision of St. John must include all nations, all languages and all peoples.

Mendieta surmised that since both the Jews and Muslims had prior knowledge of the scripture, their conversion should be relatively easy. The Gentiles, on the other hand, had no prior knowledge of the word of God and thus posed the greatest challenge. In the Luke parable, the host sent his servant to take to the streets and "make them come in"; Mendieta read this to mean that the pagan population of the Americas had to be converted by force if necessary. This meant a strong paternal presence rather than violence: "The Gentiles should be compelled in the sense of being guided by the power and the authority of fathers who have the faculty to discipline their children."

The imposition of that authority took many forms, with mixed results. In the end, the Nahuas and their neighbors played as much of a role in the conversion process as did the friars and other Spanish priests; the result was the formation not just of a Mexican Catholicism but of many localized Catholicisms. The key point here is that embedded in that process were millenarian ideas such as those articulated by Mendieta. The friars believed that their primary role was to prepare the inhabitants of the new continent for the impending coming of Christ.

To make the point another way, take the example of the mission complex at Actopan, a small Nahua town in central Mexico. It was built by Augustinians, not Franciscans, but the ideological impetus behind it was the same—the friars chose millennialism as the central theme used to adorn the walls of the church's open chapel (figure 21), making sure that apocalyptic imagery permeated the visual world of their indigenous flock. Built in the 1550s, the open chapel was the

21. The Open Chapel of Actopan, Mexico, sixteenth century.

first completed permanent architecture in the mission town and was where most public masses were held. The structure was not unique to Actopan; in fact, these open chapels were invented to accommodate the large numbers of indigenous congregants who could not easily fit into the relatively small naves of New World mission churches. Open chapels were thus a standard architectural form used throughout New Spain during the early years of the evangelical campaigns, before warfare and epidemic disease reduced the indigenous populations to such levels that even the small interiors of the mission churches could accommodate entire villages.

The open chapel of Actopan is impressive, indeed. It is a relatively simple design, consisting of a monumental barrel vault that terminates in a sheer back wall, forming a massive niche. Halfway up the rear wall of the open chapel a friar would have stood on a raised podium that hosted a small altar. The lack of paintings on the rear wall most likely approximates the location and size of this platform. From this lofty stage the priest would have delivered stirring, apocalyptic messages to the crowd below.

While the words of the friar's sermons were an ephemeral oration, whose subtleties have been lost in the intervening centuries, the visual culture that surrounds this architectural context provides a permanent record of the sermons' probable themes. The vertical walls of the open chapel are completely covered in multicolored murals that vividly illustrated the themes of the priests' sermons. One can easily imagine an Augustinian friar using the murals as didactic aids, using a long stick to point out specific visual moments to drive his point home to the congregants. The use of "public" art was particularly necessary early in the Spiritual Conquest, when most of the indigenous population could not understand Spanish, let alone Latin. The Actopan murals are silent testaments to the Spanish priests' obsession with the impending Apocalypse—and to their efforts to scare their new flock into believing, too.

The walls of the open chapel were divided into a gridded pattern with individual scenes inhabiting the created rectilinear spaces. This was probably a deliberate imitation of the native painting style seen in pre-Columbian codices. Viewed as a whole, the mural cycle is a morality tale demonstrating proper behavior for the newly Christianized Nahua parishioners. Some scenes are banal enough—there are images that promote Christian marriage, for example—but the majority of the mural cycle is devoted to gruesome imaginings. The context of these more violent images is the millennial and apocalyptic flavor of the New World evangelical campaign, as the paintings form an elaborate version of the Last Judgment. While the priest preached of the agonies that awaited the unconverted, the unbelieving, or even the misbehaving neophyte, he was surrounded by horrific scenes of torture, painted to scare the local population into submission to the new religion. On the walls are people with brown skin—clearly intended to represent the local Nahuas—being subjected to a variety of tortures; the techniques were the tried-and-true torments of medieval Europe, such as flaying, burning, and stretching on flaming racks.

One scene is particularly harrowing. It is now badly faded, but enough of it can be seen (see figure 22): It depicts a massive gaping mouth, an immense, blue maw reminiscent of the medieval Hell-

22. *The Maws of Hell* mural, Actopan, Mexico, sixteenth century.

mouth seen in chapter 3, but here reimagined especially for a native audience. It is to this scene that the priest would have pointed as he explained in full detail the lasting consequence of un-Christian behavior. On the day of reckoning, one could only expect to be ush-ered into the depths of hell for all eternity—and for the friars who led the Spiritual Conquest in the New World, that Day of Judgment was coming soon. The message was clear: be afraid; be very afraid.

$\sim$

We left Moctezuma, earlier in the chapter, yellow-bellied and paralyzed by superstition, but with a promise to rehabilitate his reputation. We argued above that two sets of contextual evidence undermine the notion that the Aztec emperor was lily-livered: the lack of a strong millenarian or apocalyptic tradition in central Mexican culture and Moctezuma's aggressive, expansionist track record during the seventeen years of his rule leading up to the Spanish invasion. Sure enough, a closer look at the sources that painted the image of Moctezuma as a tragic millenarianist date from after that invasion; the portrait is a post-Conquest creation, with roots more in medieval Europe than Aztec Mexico.

For example, in the various versions of the speech that Moctezuma allegedly made to Cortés, the emphasis is on political sovereignty, not the millenarian fulfillment of a religious idea. In the larger passage from which we quoted earlier, Cortés makes no mention of Quetzalcoatl (who does not appear in any of Cortés's five letters to the king), nor does he ever claim that Moctezuma took him for a god. Bernal Díaz del Castillo, a conquistador who witnessed the famous meeting, repeats Cortés' account without mention of any gods. Likewise, the Nahua account in the Florentine Codex neither names any deities nor suggests that Cortés is one.

However, in a mid-sixteenth century account by Francisco López de Gómara (not a conquistador but Cortés' secretary in Spain), Mexican natives initially imagine that all Spaniards are gods. Gómara's influential account introduced a number of themes and twists to the tale that are picked up and turned into conventional wisdom for centuries—the apotheosis of the conquistadors is one of them. Furthermore, the notion of Cortés as the returning lord, with its biblical echoes in the tales of the Prodigal Son and the Second Coming, was seized upon by Spanish chroniclers and soon became firmly entrenched in Conquest narratives.

Scholars of Nahuatl, the language spoken by the Aztecs, and the Aztec culture of reverential or polite speech, agree that Moctezuma's speech reads as a regal and gracious welcome, not a surrender. Whether Cortés simply misunderstood—via his interpreters—or deliberately twisted the words of the emperor is not clear. But his interpretation made sound political sense. It was a report written to the king at a moment in the two-year war when the invasion was faltering; to depict the meeting with the emperor as a surrender that was reminiscent of the Muslim surrender of Granada to the Spanish king in 1492, despite the fact that Cortés had been violently expelled from the Aztec capital and half his men slaughtered, was pure spin.

But it was not just Cortés' political instincts and the jingoism of subsequent Spanish writers that cemented the tale of Moctezuma's surrender. Before long, another group of Spaniards—the Franciscans in Mexico—began to promote the notion that Cortés was a divine agent, God's medium for bringing the faith to Mexico. "Through this captain, God opened the door for us to preach his holy gospel," one of the Twelve, Motolinía (his name was taken from the Nahuatl for "poverty"), told the king. "Who has loved and defended the Indians of this new world like Cortés?" Motolinía was one of the first to spread the story that native Mexicans called the Spanish invaders gods, later adding the detail that Cortés was taken for Quetzalcoatl; it showed that the Mexicans had anticipated the Spaniards, hoping for their arrival in some sense, and that the Conquest was thus part of God's plan for the world.

The Nahuatl text quoted above, taken from the Florentine Codex, was itself influenced in various ways by the Franciscan millenarian vision of the Conquest, including the privileged role of Cortés within that narrative. The Codex was the life's work of another early Franciscan in Mexico, Bernardino de Sahagún. He arrived in 1529 and worked on the project's twelve bilingual (Spanish-Nahuatl) volumes from 1547 into the 1580s. In 1579 he supervised the composition of the Nahuatl account of the Conquest but rewrote it five years later to greater magnify and glorify Cortés' providential role.

Viewed from either perspective—the Nahua account or the Franciscan one—Cortés comes off well and Moctezuma poorly. This is partly because the Nahua version was composed by men from Tlatelolco, a neighborhood of the Aztec capital city of Tenochtitlán, one that was once a separate town and that held out the longest during the brutal siege of 1520–1521. Moctezuma was not a Tlatelolcan; decades after his death and the empire's demise, he became a convenient target for Tlatelolcans keen to explain defeat while saving community face. Thus Moctezuma the nervous, hesitant, cowardly ruler, terrorized by omens and kowtowing to the Spaniards, is fully present in the Codex (see figure 23, an illustration from the Codex Durán). Seeming to be true, simply by virtue of being the view of the vanquished, the portrait is a Tlatelolcan-Franciscan invention, deeply infused with millenarian themes.

Even the omens that supposedly unnerved the emperor upon the eve of the invention were introduced by Motolinia in the 1540s. They seem indigenous enough—a comet over the Mexican night sky,

23. Moctezuma, from the Codex Durán, 1581.

a temple bursts into flames, another hit by lightning, the water on Lake Texcoco boils, a crane with a mirror on its head caught in the lake. Yet all have been traced back to three ancient Mediterranean sources (by Plutarch, Lucan, and Josephus), classical works taught in the College of Santa Cruz set up by Franciscans in Tlatelolco to educate young Nahua noblemen. The original omens predict the falls of Jerusalem and Rome; for native Tlatelolocans and Franciscan friars alike, pre-Conquest Tenochtitlán was an ill-fated New World Rome and Jerusalem. And as the omens acquired Aztec details and merged with local fables, they too acquired a veneer of authenticity.

As Cortés' legend took form and solidified, so did Moctezuma's role as scapegoat for the Aztec defeat take clearer shape—the flip side of the same coin. That coin was minted by the Franciscans, keen to maintain their vision of the New World as an opportunity to create on earth a version of the "New Jerusalem" described in the Book of Revelation. As a result, the history of the Conquest of Mexico was revised and reimagined, and Aztec culture infused with the Franciscans' millenarian spirit, as symbolized by the ill treatment given to the emperor's reputation. The story of how that process played out among the Maya—who were themselves faced with Franciscan friars not long after Moctezuma's death—is the focus of the next chapter.

· 5 ·

Apocalypto

The Millennium Comes to the Maya

"A great and wondrous sign appeared in heaven: a woman clothed with the sun, with the moon under her feet and a crown of twelve stars on her head."

—The Book of Revelation 12:1

"Ask a devout Maya and he might answer in words which sound very much like a prophecy, 'The Cross sleeps.' And as the reader knows, that which sleeps might also awaken."

—from the prologue to Hubert Smith's 2009 novel,
Maya Apocalypse: A Nelson Cocom Thriller

"These characters have to be utterly believable as pre-Columbian Mesoamericans."

—Mel Gibson, on the Maya protagonists
of his 2006 movie, *Apocalypto*

In 1549, at the young age of twenty-five, Diego de Landa set out on an adventure that would define the rest of his life. Having become a Franciscan friar eight years earlier in Spain, he joined a new expedition of three other young priests sailing for the New World. Their mission was to assist his order's massive Catholic conversion of the

24. Frederick Catherwood, *Ruins at Izamal*, 1844.

indigenous population of the Americas. Led by an older Franciscan friar named Lorenzo de Bienvenida, Landa was sent to the province of Yucatan. This small colony in the northwest of the peninsula of that name was considered perilous and challenging; the province's capital of Merida had only been founded seven years earlier, the dust was still settling after twenty years of invasion warfare, and colonial rule outside a few Spanish towns had yet to be firmly established.

The two priests, Landa and Bienvenida, were assigned to missionize in the Chel region of the peninsula—east of Merida in a former kingdom where most of the local people had yet to see a Spanish priest, let alone be converted to Christianity. They were expected to establish a mission town at an appropriate locale, a base from which to spread the word.

After traveling through the region for several months, the duo came upon the ancient Maya metropolis of Itzmal. Although the town's population was a fraction of what it had been a thousand years earlier, and many of its older structures lay in ruins, Itzmal was still inhabited and—most importantly—still functioned as a major Maya pilgrimage site. At its peak in early Classic times, Itzmal had been a monumental city, consisting of numerous vast pyramids, sparkling paved plazas, and large-scale public artwork (seen here in figure 24, a nineteenth-century lithograph of a stucco sculpture that once decorated the side of a building). Straight, raised, white roads (called *sacbeob*) linked the city to other important sites in the peninsula, such as neighboring Aké.

The chief object of the pilgrimages to the pyramids of the town was the native deity Itzamnaaj, the god of shamanism, knowledge, and healing. Inspired by the sacred status of the town, Bienvenida and Landa began construction of a monumental church and monastery, erecting a Christian building directly on top of the Maya pyramid known to have originally housed Maya priests dedicated to the Itzamnaaj cult. Over the course of the next two decades the church complex became the most elaborate in the province, eventually situating itself as the "jewel" of the Franciscan evangelical campaign. The complex was positioned sixteen feet above plaza level on the base of the original pyramid (seen in figure 25). In its finished form (which it had reached by the mid-seventeenth century), the complex consisted of a barrel-vaulted nave church, two double-storied cloisters, and a 1,000-square-foot atrium (seen in figure 26). This scale was an impressive feat by any colonial standards, but particularly so in the relatively poor province of Yucatan.

The church's success stemmed partly from the ingenuity of Landa himself. Recognizing the site's sacred importance to the Maya population, he installed a carved Virgin Mary in the church, who for all intents and purposes began to take on the religious roles held by Itzamnaaj in the previous centuries. She was a healing Virgin, acclaimed to have numinous powers, and within a matter of years was visited by thousands of pilgrims annually. Landa's foresight was clearly well grounded; today, the Virgin of Itzmal is the patron saint of the Yucatan Peninsula.

25. The pre-Columbian pyramidal base of the monastic complex of Itzmal, Yucatan, Mexico.

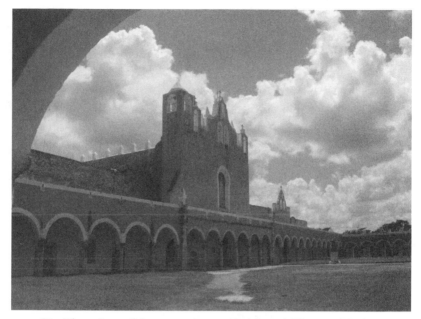

26. The atrium of the monastic complex, Itzmal, Yucatan, Mexico.

As part of the original building program, executed a decade or so after the church's completion in the 1560s, Maya artists painted a series of murals. In the small room that led from the open expanse of the atrium and into the semiprivate space of the cloister, the local artists completed a multicolor scene that wrapped around the small room's walls, reaching from floor to ceiling. The murals are now heavily deteriorated due to the province's humid climate, but the scenes have survived sufficiently to lend insight into the reasoning behind the heavy investment placed in the conversion campaign by the Franciscans in Mexico and Yucatan (indeed, by all the religious orders in the New World—not just the Franciscans, but also the Dominicans, Augustinians, and later the Jesuits, too).

On the left wall a pastoral scene is apparent. Franciscan friars, identifiable due to their long brown robes and tonsured heads, mingle in a landscape reminiscent of the Yucatan itself, with its low-lying shrub forests. Among the priests, Maya neophytes themselves participate in the peaceful scene, wandering among the Franciscans, playing drums, collecting honey, and—perhaps most significantly—engaging in penitent rituals.

Across the small room, the murals on the opposite wall are opposite in intention (figure 27). Here, the scene is not one of peaceful respite but instead is imbued with violence. Less legible than the left wall, the right wall still clearly depicts a troubled landscape. Red-skinned beings appear to beat objects with long poles. Like the idyllic scene across the room, this violent action seems to take place in the Yucatan, as similar trees have been included to give the audience a notion of place. It easily brings to mind the gruesome scenes, visited in the previous chapter, that decorate the walls of the open chapel at Actopan.

While these oppositional scenes could easily be read as a "good

27. *The "Devil" mural*, Itzmal, Yucatan, Mexico.

Indian/bad Indian" cautionary tale, another part of the mural cycle hints at the real significance of the paintings. On the east wall—the wall that connects the pastoral and demon paintings—a doorway leads directly into the cloister. Here, placed right above the doorjamb, a diminutive image of the Virgin was painted. She is small, but she cannot be missed: one must walk right beneath her to enter the cloister (only later would she be bypassed by pilgrims wishing to pay homage to the Virgin of Itzmal in her private chapel located behind the church's nave and only accessible through the cloister); and one's attention is grabbed by the bright hues that the Maya artist no doubt deliberately selected. Painted in a traditional red and blue robe, and then set against a vibrant yellow orb, this was no neutral or ordinary painting of the Virgin Mary. The Maya artists, undoubtedly under the direction of Itzmal's resident Franciscan priests, had painted the Virgin of the Apocalypse.

As discussed earlier, the Virgin of the Apocalypse references a section of the New Testament's Book of Revelations in which the Second Coming of Christ is prophesied. "A great and wondrous sign appeared in heaven," wrote John, in the passages that inspired Dürer's famous print series. A signal of the impending Apocalypse, according to John's vision, there appeared "a woman clothed with the sun, with the moon under her feet and a crown of twelve stars on her head." Placed in the context of the monumental Itzmal monastery, and situated between the pastoral and devil murals, this small Virgin of the Apocalypse was far larger in import than her diminutive portrait suggests. She not only referenced the Doomsday warnings of Revelation but also she provided justification for the entirety of the conversion campaigns launched in the New World. In short, the efforts of the friars were justified and urgent; the souls of the Maya had to be saved soon, so as to be prepared—or more, so as to hasten—the Second Coming of Christ and the accompanying Apocalypse.

Landa's personal zeal for this millennial task continued to mount. After a dozen years proselytizing the Maya and supervising the transformation of Itzmal, the Spanish friar was called away to Merida.

There he was promoted to head or "provincial" of the Franciscans in Yucatan, and as such he soon heard rumors of recidivism in Maya villages; that is, efforts by local men to maintain traditional "pagan" rituals and practices after the community had supposedly been converted to Christianity. In the spring of 1562, two young Maya boys outside of the town of Mani, the headquarters of the Franciscan evangelical campaign, accidentally came upon a cache of ceramic sculptures and human skulls collected in a cave. The youths immediately returned to the village and described their discovery to the local priest. He ordered the cached objects brought into the church's atrium and commanded the Maya who lived close to the cave to come to Mani for questioning. They quickly admitted to using the objects to petition the native deities for rain, confessing that this was still a common local practice.

The Franciscan response was to bring down on the Maya a virtual apocalypse; within months, Mani became the epicenter of a full scale Inquisition, led by Landa himself. Surrounding villages were ordered to turn over sculptures of native deities (termed *idolos* by the Catholic priests, classifying them as Satanic superstition) and pre-Columbian books. All items were burned in massive bonfires in Mani. Thousands of Maya were arrested and questioned under the threat of torture. Many were put to torment on the pulley and the *burro*, a wooden rack to which victims were tied. As many as two hundred died during the summer months, hundreds more were left permanently scarred or crippled, and dozens appear to have committed suicide to avoid the agonies of Inquisition interrogations.

For the Maya of Mani and neighboring towns, 1562 was an end-of-world date, the long summer a harrowing series of Judgment Days. Indeed, a famous modern representation of the 1562 Inquisition portrays it in Doomsday hues. The second floor of the Palacio de Gobierno, on the northern edge of Merida's colonial plaza, is decorated with a mural cycle detailing Yucatec history from the pre-Columbian to the modern eras. Viewed by thousands of local inhabitants, schoolchildren, and foreign tourists each year, these images have become paradigmatic of the province's defining historical moments, perhaps shaping public opinion more than any ancient, colonial, or modern textual source. In the scene that depicts that violent summer in Mani, Landa himself is depicted not as a beneficent protector of the Maya—as his writings composed during his exile to Spain to wait trial for his part in the Inquisition would have us believe—but as an evil torturer (figure 28).

28. Fernando Castro Pacheco, *Diego de Landa and the Mani Inquisition of 1562.*

A mostly monochromatic scene composed of oranges and gray-scale, Landa inhabits a full third of the composition. Poised above a vast fire in which carved statues of Maya deities can be seen succumbing to the tall flames, he presides over a figurative "end of the world," as the events were surely understood by the Maya. The Franciscan seems to be of the flames himself, the ashes, as he holds the Bible in his right hand, the ultimate justification for the unmediated violence, and a burning pole in his left, proclaiming his ultimate culpability for this tragedy. His facial expression is stern and unmoving, providing modern viewers a transparent, if perhaps overly stated, understanding of his religious convictions.

~

These moments from the first dozen years of Spiritual Conquest in Yucatan—the missionary zeal of Landa, the murals and structures of Itzmal, the apocalyptic summer of 1562—are vivid symbols of the millenarian determination of the Franciscans to convert the Maya. In the Maya world as a whole, that process proved to be a protracted and complex one—begun in the late 1520s in Guatemala and stretching across the centuries of colonial rule into the modern period. Just as conversion efforts in central Mexico resulted in local Nahua versions of Catholicism, so did Maya Catholicisms emerge in colonies such as Yucatan.

One feature of the local form of Catholicism forged in Yucatan by Franciscans and Maya neophytes was millennial ideology—not simply imposed upon or injected into the Maya worldview, but appropriated by Maya elders, scribes, and religious officials. In chapter 1, we discussed the tale of the destruction of the world from the *Book of the Chilam Balam of Chumayel*, primarily using the passage that one translator named "the ceremonial of the *baktun*" and another named "the creation of the world." Having deliberately presented this material in such a way as to emphasize the supposedly "pure" indigenous apocalyptic nature of these texts, we now revisit them, placing them more fully within the historical and cultural context in which they were written and rewritten. Viewed as such, these passages tell a drastically different story, one in which Franciscan millennial ideology plays a far more prominent role than 2012ologists would have us believe. These seemingly "Maya" passages are in fact directly channeled from medieval European preoccupations with the end of the world.

One of the contributors to the Chumayel manuscript—a late-seventeenth century Maya scribe who goes unnamed—wrote into the book a twenty-page summary of Maya "mythistory." This ranged from texts detailing the origins of the ancient gods to the creation of human beings to calendrical rituals of his own day (we quoted from it in chapter 1). Much of it was no doubt copied from earlier alphabetic versions of ancient glyphic texts, such as the Dresden Codex. But much of it was influenced by Christianity, directly drawn from sources brought to Yucatan by Franciscan friars.

The creation-of-the-world narrative is an example of this Maya blending of European material with local traditions. The reworking of the old Oxlahuntiku/Bolontiku myth so that it concludes with a Christian-style Apocalypse obviously made sense to the colonial-era Maya scribe. As we saw in chapter 1, the destruction of the world is presented as a cosmic battle between the deities associated with the celestial realm and the Underworld, Oxlahuntiku and Bolontiku. Bolontiku destroys Oxlahuntiku, heaping upon him a series of abuses until his rain god aspect is removed from the heavens. This sets the stage for a monumental flood that destroys—or will destroy—the world.

Immediately after Oxlahuntiku's destruction, however, the world flowers with a variety of edible plant species. This destruction/creation sequence, culminating in the flowering of the next era, parallels Maya agricultural techniques of slash and burn, whereby the naturally occurring flora of a *milpa* (cornfield) must be destroyed for more useful plants to be cultivated and flourish. After the mythic flowering, the corn plant is stolen away, resulting in the collapse of the world. Cosmic destruction is ushered in by the anticipated deluge. Whether read as "a rush of rain, one sharp burst of rain" (our translation) or "one fetching of rain, one lancing of rain" (as one Maya scholar has it), the phrase hints at the violence of the apocalyptic flood as it wipes out the "heartless people." The deities called the *bacabob* (the Bacabs) then reestablish the geographical limits of the world's horizontal plane, setting up a colored tree in each of the four corners and in the center of the universe.

The details of the story have obvious pre-Columbian roots, and the agricultural metaphor is likewise highly localized. But the apocalyptic tone suggests the Book of Revelation, an impression confirmed by the passage that immediately follows. Here we defer to the translation by Timothy Knowlton (an anthropologist who specializes in colonial period Maya creation mythology):

> And thus the word of this *katun* may be accomplished / And then it was given by Dios / A deluge occurs for the second time / This is the destruction of the world / Then this ends / That Our Lord who is Jesus Christ may then descend / Upon the valley of Jehoshaphat beside the town of Jerusalem / It occurred that he redeems us by his holy blood.

The references to the Apocalypse and the Second Coming are explicit; but do we know exactly how they made their way into Maya alphabetic writings composed far away from overseeing friars and for specifically Maya-only purposes? Knowlton has determined that two versions of a popular European account of apocalyptic lore were translated into Yucatec Mayan during the colonial period. This text, titled *Fifteen Signs before Doomsday*, appears in the *Book of the Chilam Balam* kept by the village of Tusik, and in another Maya text that scholars call the Morley Manuscript (a little-studied text that is akin to a *Chilam Balam* book). Of these fifteen signs, the first is a global flood that leads to the Last Judgment.

Of particular relevance to our argument here is the fact that the prophesy of the Second Coming of Christ is the climax to these Maya passages. This was not inserted to mollify Spanish priests; Europeans were never intended to see the highly guarded, clandestine books written by and exclusively for Maya authors and readers. In fact, the Maya of Chumayel, Tusik, and other villages could safely assume that if a Franciscan happened to stumble upon the manuscript, they would have destroyed it; the friars continued to burn suspect texts of Maya authorship for some two hundred years after Landa's great Inquisition bonfire of 1562. So how then can these explicit references to Christianity be explained? We cannot assume that they were afterthoughts merely tacked on to the end of an otherwise purely Maya creation story because they were deemed "interesting" or perhaps "innovative" to the Maya authors.

On the contrary, Christian passages and ideas permeate the entire *Chilam Balam* text. For example, the flood and subsequent creation of the world is itself presided over by a Christian, not Maya, protagonist. This is not made clear in the classic translation of the passage by the late Ralph Roys: "There would be a sudden rush of water when the theft of the insignia [of Oxlahuntiku] occurred. Then the sky would fall, it would fall down upon the earth, when the four gods, the four Bacabs, were set up, who brought about the destruction of the world." However, the supposedly Mayan word that Roys translated as "insignia"—*cangel*—is in other Maya documents used as a version of "Archangel." The difference may seem small—a case of Mayanists arguing over minutiae. But it actually transforms the passage into a highly hybridized account of creation, in which directly following the Flood, the Archangel of the cornfield arrives to oversee the setting up of the new creation.

Dissatisfied with Roys's version, a later scholar, the late Munro Edmonson, reinterpreted the Oxlahuntiku creation story as a passage about the calendar. The result was a kind of chain reaction that resulted in a further misrepresentation used to support the supposed 2012 evidence found in colonial Maya sources. In chapter 1, we quoted Edmonson's translation and comments on the "millennial words" that marked the celebration in Merida of the *baktun* ending in

1618. The impression that Edmonson gives, and which we deliberately echoed, was that as recently as the start of the current *baktun*—which ends in December 2012—the Maya were still ritually celebrating the four-hundred-year cycle; indeed, he states bluntly that the Long Count lasted this late. In the decades since Edmonson translated *The Chilam Balam of Chumayel*, this impression has been cited numerous times and has worked its way into the fabric of Maya calendar studies and 2012ology.

It is, however, misleading. The passage does *not* record a Long Count date, nor is there any evidence in this or any of the *Chilam Balam* books that the Maya were still maintaining the Long Count of Classic times. The passage does not describe a *baktun*, or ever use the term; the book refers only to the *tun* (the solar year) and the twenty-year cycle of the *katun*. It was Edmonson himself, not the Maya authors, who dubbed the passage *The Ceremonial of the Baktun*; in the original manuscript, it has no title, unless one counts the title on the previous page, *Quinto: 1620* (Fifth: 1620). Edmonson dismisses this, unconvincingly, as "a late addition," but close examination of the handwritings reveals it to have been written by the same person (see figure 29). The passage in fact describes the ritual ending of a *katun* cycle, but because that cycle happened to be the final one in a *baktun*, Edmonson inferred (in effect, invented) the larger "ceremony."

As for the text itself, it is heavily imbued with the influences of Christian and Spanish culture. One of the officials at the ritual is described as being *Antachristo* (the Antichrist, representing the Maya who refuse to convert to Christianity), and the presiding officer claims to be called *Ceçar Agusto* (Caesar Augustus). There is no corroborating evidence to prove these ceremonies actually took place in Merida in 1618 or 1620. But assuming they did, they represented a stage in the centuries-long process whereby the rituals that marked the old Maya calendar were reconciled to the rituals of the Christian calendar. The result in modern times (that is, roughly the past century and a half) is a hybrid set of rituals. Some of these have clear ancient Maya roots (like the Chachac ceremony marking the onset of the

29. Folio 49v from the *Book of the Chilam Balam of Chumayel*.

rains; Chac is an old rain god), some look like old rituals heavily colonized by Christianity (Good Friday replacing the earlier ritual of Sacrifices).

How does it relate to 2012ology? There are three key points regarding this *Chilam Balam* source. First, it is a speculative stretch to read it as being focused on the celebration of a *baktun* cycle, as representing ongoing Maya concerns with a calendar marked by beginnings and endings in 1224, 1618, and 2012. Second, to interpret the language as "millennial" is to add an implication of specific apocalyptic awareness and expectation—not just a knowledge of Second Coming ideology, but a timetable for it—that is not in the original text. Third, while we can detect ancient Maya and early modern Christian elements in the passage, it is ultimately best understood as colonial-period Maya literature, written by people who saw their culture not as piecemeal, a patchwork of two contributing cultures, but as something singular, coherent, traditional, and local—as theirs.

Why did the Maya intellectuals in the colonial period intentionally incorporate Christian theologies into their cosmologies by choice? And more specifically, why were Christian accounts of the Apocalypse so appealing to these Maya authors, when for thousands of years a nonmillennial creation mythology had successfully served the needs of the Maya culture? As Knowlton has stated, "The Christian apocalypse made sense to Colonial Maya scribes within the context of an otherwise Postclassic mythic narrative itself." In other words, when Christianity was introduced to the Yucatec Maya, they intentionally adopted aspects that could most easily be dovetailed into their preexisting worldview. The mixing of the two contributing ideologies resulted in a third cultural system, completely independent of the original two.

Recall that ancient Mesoamerican cultures conceived of time as largely cyclical, divided and charted in a series of interlocking cycles of varying lengths. They also saw creation and recreation as a continual cycle, with previous worlds stretching out behind our own current lived reality, as having occurred three or four times previously. With this as a starting point, it is easy to see how Christian accounts of the Apocalypse, with the Second Coming of Christ and the creation of a new world, would have made a "New Jerusalem" appealing to a Maya audience. In the new reality of their colonial world—thousands of native peoples felled by disease, tried and punished for their religious beliefs, forcibly removed from land they had inhabited for centuries— there must have been some kind of comfort in finding links between their traditional worldviews and those being forced upon them by Catholic priests. The incorporation of Christian themes was not necessarily a succumbing to colonial forces; it can also be seen as a socially savvy way to *maintain* cultural continuity amid the psychological trauma of the early colonial period. Apocalyptic narratives and their associated millennial theology were an ideal avenue through which converted Maya could make sense of the violence and cultural upheavals of the Spanish conquest and its chaotic aftermath.

The colonial Maya literature, the *Books of Chilam Balam*, thus tells us much about Maya history and culture. But it does not support the notion that the Maya anticipated 2012 with any sort of anxiety, if at all, either before the Spanish Conquest or after it. On the contrary, it shows how Spanish Franciscan views of Christianity influenced the Maya intellectual landscape, infusing some European millenarian concerns into their indigenous perception of creation and time.

∾

What happened to this imported Maya millenarian tradition? As a product of the colonial encounter of the sixteenth through eighteenth centuries, did it die out when Yucatan ceased to be a Spanish colony in 1821? And if it did not die out, is there a thread of continuity through to Maya-based 2012ology?

As it turned out, Maya millenarianism *did* survive the end of colonial rule and manifested itself in a way that was vibrant, violent, and distinct to the Maya of the Yucatan. In ways that would have shocked the Franciscans of earlier centuries, the millenarian ideas they had introduced came to the fore within the context of the peninsula's prolonged nineteenth-century civil conflict dubbed the Caste War. Although the war began in 1847 as a political and regional struggle, with Hispanic and Maya protagonists on both sides, it soon evolved into a kind of race war. Most fascinatingly—and most significantly for our story—one group of Maya rebels maintained an independent state in the east into the twentieth century, ruled by a religious-political government that became known as the Cult of the Talking Cross.

While the northwest section of the peninsula had been heavily influenced by a strong Spanish presence since the earliest days of contact in the sixteenth century, the eastern half of the peninsula remained largely uncolonized for three hundred years. Brief forays were made into these wilds by Franciscans and other Spaniards—motivated primarily by commercial interests—but for the most part the Maya of this region maintained a fairly traditional way of life. Spanish maps called the region *despoblado* ("uninhabited"), which of course it was not. A major Spanish conquest expedition against independent Maya in the 1690s largely bypassed the kingdoms of the east in order to destroy the larger Itzá Maya kingdom in northern Guatemala.

This is not to say that the Maya of the eastern peninsula were not impacted by Franciscan ideologies or the Spanish colonization. On the contrary, they undoubtedly were; but unlike Maya communities to the west, the eastern Maya were largely independent and free to incorporate specific aspects of the new religion into their traditional worldview on their own terms. The entire culture of these eastern villages can thus be likened to the self-conscious incorporations of relevant biblical material into the clandestine, Maya-authored *Books of the Chilam Balam* discussed earlier.

Problems began to arise in the peninsula in the early nineteenth century, in the wake of the wars that led to Mexican independence from Spain. Regional rivalries, political factionalism within the ruling Hispanic elite, disputes over whether Yucatan should be part of the Mexican republic of an independent nation—these conflicts ensnared attempts by Maya elders to protect communal lands from private incursion. What ensued was a complex half-century of sporadic warfare that pitted the underprivileged Maya population against the powerful Hispanic elite. While the fight may have begun as a messy political endeavor, it was soon transformed into a social and racial war that eventually took on religious dimensions.

Early on in the war's history, in 1850, the Maya leaders of the rebel movement in the east established a new headquarters at a *cenote* (a natural sinkhole) called Chan Santa Cruz, Little Sacred Cross. Near the cave a large mahogany tree grew, upon which was carved an image of a cross, lending the site its name. A native religious cult emerged centered on veneration of this cross, quickly gaining support among the indigenous rebels. A sanctuary was built nearby to house the religious icon referred to as X-Balam Na, the Jaguar House, now largely destroyed.

Shortly after the Jaguar House was built, the cross began to "speak" to the local Maya. Historical records later revealed that the Cross had several interpreters who voiced the Cross's concerns and petitions. This Talking Cross soon became highly influential. It urged the Maya not to end their battle with the Spanish population, "Because it has come / The time / For an Indian Uprising / Over the Whites / Once and for all." Through his interpreters, the Talking Cross offered God's protection, even promising them invincibility in battle. The cult's followers were called the Cruzob (the Spanish for "cross" with a Mayan plural, -*ob*).

Despite the power of the Talking Cross, many Cruzob rebels lost their lives in the attacks and skirmishes that followed. The Hispanic state's mixed-race army then moved on Chan Santa Cruz, stealing the Cross and killing one of its interpreters, a rebel leader named Manuel Nauat. But millenarian belief often proves resistant to disappointment, and this was as much the case in nineteenth-century Yucatan as elsewhere. The rebel Maya simply installed a new Cross to replace the confiscated original, with the new one communicating in writing via the assistance of a handful of scribes. There was also a group of smaller, proxy crosses, carried into battle for divine protection. Like the Talking Cross, the proxies tended to be draped in an *ipil* (or *huipil*), the traditional garment worn by Maya women. This was a Christian cross, its symbolic power derived from the faith introduced three centuries earlier by Franciscans; but the cult had a distinctly Maya identity, forged by Maya to serve a local movement, the cause of the Cruzob.

Eventually, the strife faded and fizzled out. In 1901 the Mexican army advanced again on Chan Santa Cruz, taking it without a fight, occupying it and the surrounding Maya villages. The international border to the south, between Mexico and Belize, had been formalized in the previous decade, eventually resulting in the creation of a new Mexican state, Quintana Roo. But resentments, hostilities, and even millenarian expectations persisted. The eastern half of the Yucatan peninsula remained relatively dangerous for non-Maya peoples well into the twentieth century—the last recognized skirmish was recorded in 1933, giving the Caste War a total span of some eighty-five years. As late as the 1960s, Maya elders in the east expressed an expectation that an outsider would bring guns and encourage the Cruzob to rise up again.

And today? What has become of this seemingly isolated outpost of the Spanish Empire? Has the Cruzob cause seized upon the imminence of 2012 and emerged again to prepare the Maya for apocalypse and renewal? Are there any direct lines of influence and ideology between the ancient Maya of the Long Count, the Cruzob Maya of eastern Yucatan, and the 2012 phenomenon?

In short, no; there is no such direct line. Instead, the lines of influence run from medieval Christianity to colonial and Caste War–era Yucatan, and in parallel (not in series) from that same medieval source to the modern phenomenon of interpreting the ancient Long Count to serve 2012ology. Ironically, the eastern coast of the peninsula has witnessed a Maya resurgence, but hardly the kind imagined by Cruzob elders. While the ancient Maya have been appropriated by 2012ologists (admittedly, in a spirit of profound appreciation), international and Mexican business interests have appropriated the ancient Maya (in a spirit of exploitation) in order to dramatically refigure the east into a tourist zone. They have named it the "Riviera Maya."

Centered around the modern development of Isla Cancún (as opposed to colonial Cancún, located a few miles inland), a largely North American and European tourist base can enjoy the natural splendor of the Yucatan's east coast at scores of hotels and eco-resorts. For those visitors willing to take a break from suntanning, snorkeling, zip lining, and wet T-shirt contests, numerous agencies are set up to bring curious tourists on trips farther south and inland to fully restored ancient Maya sites. The most accessible are Chichén Itzá and Tulum, but the efforts of archaeologists and road crews are gradually putting more cities in range.

The 2012 phenomenon is expected to give such tourism a boost, and various end-of-world celebrations and expeditions are planned. One of these—a further twist of irony, in view of the argument laid out in this chapter—is an event called The Prophets Conference: 2012 Tipping Point, scheduled in Cancún for the same month as this book's publication date. The speakers, or "faculty," are prominent modern Gnostics and New Age 2012ologists who see 2012 as marking "a new birth of human consciousness" (Graham Hancock), "the beginning of a new cycle into an expanded planetary being" (Cody Johnson), "a return of the feminine" (Christine Page), and an "apocalyptic passage" through which "we will conceive ourselves, increasingly, as fractal expressions of a unified field of consciousness and sentient aspects of a planetary ecology" (Graham Pinchbeck).

"The purpose of the Maya coming to this planet was very specific," proclaims José Arguelles on The Prophets Conference website, "to leave behind a definite set of clues and information about the nature and purpose of our planet at this particular time in the solar system and in the galactic field." Or, in the more measured phrases of John Major Jenkins, the meeting of 2012ologists is "to explore a radically different, more optimistic interpretation of the Mayan prophecy—as referring to the end of the world as we have known it." How the 2012 phenomenon got to this (tipping) point—considering the ancient Maya roots and medieval Christian sources detailed in the previous chapters—is the subject of our final chapter.

· 6 ·

We Are Almost There

Why People Believe

"It may end later, but I see no reason for its ending sooner. This I mention not to assert when the time of the end shall be, but to put a stop to the rash conjectures of fancifull men who are frequently predicting the time of the end, & by doing so bring the sacred prophesies into discredit as often as their predictions fail."

—Sir Isaac Newton, predicting in 1705 that
the world would end on or after 2060

"To learn much more about the details of the end of the world, you are invited to write Family Radio . . . I Hope God Will Save Me! We Are Almost There!"

—pamphlet distributed nationally by
Family Radio, based in Oakland, California

"On December 21, 2012, the ancient Maya calendar ends. Is it a time of transition? Will the world end? Nothing at all? No one knows for sure. . . . but no matter what you believe, what better place to see in the new era, than the land of the Maya!"

—duPlooy's Jungle Lodge, Belize

$\mathcal{D}$eep in the Maya rain forests, near the border between Belize and Guatemala, is a small hotel—a "jungle lodge" bed-and-breakfast called duPlooy's. Spectacular Maya cities like Tikal are a few hours' drive away, so the lodge thrives on ancient ruins tourism. On December 18–22, 2012, duPlooy's is offering a five-day "Apocalypto" special, complete with tours of nearby Maya sites. And there's a Doomsday twist. If the lodge—and the world—still exists on the fifth night, that of December 22, your stay there is free. "If you think that we will still be here," proclaims the lodge's website, "this is a bargain. If you don't, at least you won't have to pay for the 22nd!"

You are probably smiling at this. So too, no doubt, are the owners of duPlooy's Jungle Lodge and of other hotels within range of Tikal, as their reservation books fill. So too will the Apocalypto tourists smile over their jungle breakfasts on December 22—apocalyptic hangovers aside. In the end—or rather, after the end—2012 is a smiling matter.

But it is also a seriously widespread phenomenon, a magnet for worldwide weirdness that has taken on industrial proportions. Indeed, the very extent of the 2012 phenomenon is arguably its most significant feature. Those interested in booking the Apocalypto special at duPlooy's can prepare for the trip by choosing among hundreds of books now available on 2012 predictions. Some of these publications seek to explain the phenomenon in a serious way, and many successfully debunk the myths of 2012 based on misinterpretations of astronomical patterns or of the Maya calendar. But most of the literature is built upon sensationalizing the idea that *something* will happen in 2012. *Prophecy, destiny, catastrophe, apocalypse, extinction, secret, mystery* (and yes, the *end of the world*)—these are the terms that adorn the titles of such books. There are also thousands of 2012 websites; in fact, if one includes websites not devoted entirely to the phenomenon but containing chatter about it, the number rises to tens of millions.

Thus the final, and perhaps most important, question is not whether the world will end in 2012 (it won't) or whether the Maya predicted it would (they didn't) or how millenarian ideas got into the

Maya world (Franciscan friars brought them from Europe) or what civilization most nurtured notions of the Apocalypse (it was Western, not Mesoamerican). The final question is, why do people believe in 2012?

~

Let us tackle this question by starting at the outer edges of the problem, with the more general question of why people believe in things *like* 2012; we shall then move inward toward the Western millenarian tradition, before ending where we began, with the Maya.

The belief in things *like* 2012, whether we call it belief in pseudoscience or "weird things," might be placed in two intertwined categories that are also relevant specifically to millenarianism and to 2012 speculation—optimistic and pessimistic.

"More than any other, the reason people believe weird things is because they want to," remarks Michael Shermer, a prolific writer on pseudoscience and the "borderlands" of belief ("where sense meets nonsense," as the title of one of his books puts it). Belief in weird things is "comforting" and "consoling"; it offers "immediate gratification." In other words, people believe in psychics and ghosts, UFOs and alien abductions, Atlantis and channeling, and the imminence of the Apocalypse or a new age for the same reason that people embrace religious faith. Belief offers an explanation without need for evidence. It offers a simple solution to life's complexities, a source of meaning and hope in a world of cruel whimsy and chaos.

A similar argument, put bluntly and less charitably, is that people are ignorant. A lack of education or understanding of the complexities of the Maya calendar, of the history of millenarianism in the West, or of the movements of the planets make all of us vulnerable to overly simplistic, pseudoscientific predictions. Without the specialist knowledge that 99.9 percent of the population cannot possibly acquire, it can be hard to distinguish between science and pseudoscience, evidence and faith: are evolution and global warming real? Can happy thoughts really produce happy molecules? Is 2012 real? That confusion and vulnerability has for many centuries been exploited by self-proclaimed messiahs, gurus, and cult leaders of all kinds—not to mention the racists who promote Holocaust denial, the fundamentalists who spread creationism, and the politicians who scoff at global warming. Not believing can be lonely. Embracing a position, taking a leap of faith, as nonsensical or "weird" as the belief may at first seem, can bring the comfort of belonging to a group, the reassurance of a shared belief and a common identity.

The optimistic and pessimistic beliefs are therefore like the two halves of a seesaw. With respect to 2012, the fear that the world is coming to a catastrophic end on December 21 (the pessimistic half of the mania) is balanced by the belief that the "end" is really the start of a new era of hope and enlightenment (the optimistic half). The two halves are connected, needing each other to exist. The millions of people worldwide who encounter 2012 ideas can move up and down the seesaw, finding confirmation for their pessimism about the world or reassurance that there is a future—perhaps a better one—beyond December 21.

Millenarianism in the West has also tended to take optimistic and pessimistic forms (these are our terms); both are apparent in the 2012 phenomenon. The pessimistic dwells on the end; think of it as the Four Horsemen trampling on humankind or massive earthquakes swallowing Las Vegas and Los Angeles. The optimistic is more properly called chiliasm or millennialism. As we saw in previous chapters, the Christian version holds that Christ will return again, ushering in a Paradise on earth for a thousand years (*millennial*-ism) before the Final Judgment. The nondenominational version sees the present as flawed, even disastrous, but anticipates history moving teleologically or progressively toward an ideal future. That future is sometimes based on the return of an imagined Golden Age of long ago.

Chiliasm is at the very heart of modern Western civilization, so much so that we are not even aware of it as such. It is not just manifest in more obvious ways, such as the gamut of Christian churches from Pentecostal Protestantism to Seventh-Day Adventism to Marian

Catholicism. It is also built into Marxism and free-market capitalism. Those two ideologies are rightly seen as being in opposition to each other. Yet both base their legitimacy on a claim to be the only way society can progress toward utopia, be it through class struggle, with communism as the utopian goal, or through market freedom with universal individual prosperity as the goal. Chiliastic impulses have always underpinned and driven the trajectory of the history of the United States, from evangelical fundamentalism to libertarianism, from Manifest Destiny to modern notions of American exceptionalism, from revitalization movements to the 2012 phenomenon.

The many threads of eschatology and millenarianism run so deeply and colorfully through Western civilization that the Apocalypse acts today as a common and casual reference point. It can be deployed for alarmist purposes, as with the more hysterical 2012 literature, or as the butt of parody, which is what 2012 is no doubt soon destined to become.

For example, the British magazine *The End Is Nigh* is a successful concept because its references are familiar (figure 30 is the cover of issue #3). Few readers, especially outside Britain, may know the precise origins of the sandwich-board Doomsday prophet (he walked up and down London's Oxford Street in the 1960s and 1970s, although his precursors go all the way back to Victorian days). But most will recognize him as an icon of contemporary Apocalypse anxiety. We are so accustomed to being warned that the end is imminent that phrases such as "The alien threat among us!", "Asteroids could wipe us out!", and "The Official Magazine of the Apocalypse!" are as funny as *The End Is Nigh* intends them to be.

Indeed, the movie *2012* was a hit because it worked as a lightweight, not ponderous, spectacle. Vast cities crumbled, hundreds of millions of people died, one protagonist after another suffered the loss of family members and then they themselves perished. Yet the makers of the film were able to draw on a fundamentally funny undercurrent to end-of-world fears so as to parody previous disaster flicks (including director Roland Emmerich's own). Audiences laughed not just

30. Cover for *The End Is Nigh: The Official Magazine of the Apocalypse!*, vol. 3.

because the film was (arguably) bad, or because it did not take itself too seriously, but because the end of the world has become a potentially humorous subject. As *New York Times* film reviewer, Manohla Dargis, succinctly states, *2012* is "Old Testament-style destruction served with a smile."

When in 1938 Orson Welles narrated an adaptation of H. G. Wells's *The War of the Worlds* on CBS radio, set in part as a series of news bulletins covering a Martian invasion, some audiences famously took it to be an actual news broadcast. "Radio Listeners in Panic," ran a front-page *New York Times* headline the next day. "A wave of mass hysteria seized thousands of radio listeners," the newspaper reported, when the broadcast "led thousands to believe that an interplanetary conflict had started with invading Martians spreading wide death and destruction in New Jersey and New York." The article went on to describe some of the 875 calls that were received by the *Times*'s own switchboard. A man from Dayton, Ohio, for example, phoned the newspaper desk to enquire at "What time will it be the end of the world?" Later the same evening a woman visited a New York police station with her two young children and extra clothing in tow. She planned to leave town, but New York's finest were able to convince her to stay. Today, we laugh and marvel at such public gullibility. So how did we get from taking *The War of the Worlds* seriously to laughing at *2012*?

The explanation may lie in the increasing disconnect between our civilization's tradition of millenarian expectation and the modern world of instant Internet-delivered information. As the industrial and technological revolutions have transformed the globe over the past two centuries, predictions of doom and disaster have increased, not declined. Science has not extinguished religion but has developed a complex relationship with it. The two continually merge and separate, fight and reconcile; science is the new religion, religion has become a science. The result is increased levels of both anxiety and skepticism. Hardly had the decades-long threat of nuclear holocaust abated when new anxieties emerged: global terrorism, given a haunting visual symbol in the twin towers of 9/11; global warming, with its confusingly inconsistent impact on annual climates; and Y2K, whose failure to bring catastrophe was, ironically, as alarming as it was a relief—the end was merely postponed by a dozen years.

Doomsday predictions have become the shouts of the shepherd boy, who keeps crying "Wolf!" Most villagers ignore or laugh at his warnings. But, unlike in the story, there are always a few to point out that wolves really exist—and, in the end, that they get the sheep. There are way too many Doomsday false alarms to detail here—which of course is the point. We shall restrict ourselves, therefore, to two clusters of example prophecies and predictions, those of the 1820s–1870s and the more recent spate of 1975 to the eve of 2012.

We are leaping here, like bad historians, from the sixteenth to the nineteenth centuries—but it will likely not surprise you to be told that millenarianism prospered during those centuries. Not only that, but it received a new shot of energy from Protestantism, starting with the religious revolution led by Martin Luther and others in northern Europe in the sixteenth century and spreading quickly to England and Scotland. Protestant cults embracing apocalyptic thinking with fiery zeal—from Anabaptists, Calvinists, and Puritans to Diggers, Levellers, and Ranters—flourished in the seventeenth century, first in the British Isles and the Netherlands, and then in their North American colonies. The ideological line from early New England to a Vermont farmer named William Miller, who in 1822 began proclaiming that Christ's return was imminent, is not a simple one—the history of religion in Anglo-America is complex and well studied—but it is fair to say that it is direct.

At first, nobody listened to Farmer Miller. But then his pamphlets slowly started to sell. Millerism acquired followers in other parts of the United States, then Britain and Australia. A series of end-of-world dates were chosen in 1833 and 1834, culminating on October 22. On the day of doom, thousands climbed hills or onto rooftops—some had sold all their worldly goods—and waited to be taken up to heaven. The day became known as the Great Disappointment. The anticlimax was too much to bear for some; in a sobering anticipation of the violent denouement of later millenarian cults, there was a rash of suicides. Yet the Millerite movement survived and gave birth to several new Protestant denominations, most notably the Seventh-day Adventist Church.

Millerism was merely one of the more dramatic manifestations of millenarianism in the half century from the 1820s to 1870s. The whole English-speaking world was affected, and other parts of Europe and the Americas too (as we saw with the Cult of the Talking Cross in the previous chapter), but the most fertile ground was the United States. Some cults were utopian and as political as they were religious—the Inspirationalists in Iowa, the Owenites in Indiana, and the Shakers in England and New York State.

Others contributed to the development of a sort of populist, antiestablishment academia; the heirs to that tradition are 2012olo-gists such as José Arguelles, who sees professors as jealously guarding the portals of our domain, and John Major Jenkins, who insists we run a "cliqueish" "closed shop," in which "in-house scholars" cannot say "progressive things without fear of being fired." A hundred and fifty years ago, the modern academy was in its infancy, so the lines dividing those who were "in" (university professors) and "out" (others) were still blurred. Nevertheless, the threads of Gnosticism and millenarianism can be clearly seen in late-nineteenth century scientific and pseudoscientific investigations into astronomy and astrology, electromagnetism and clairvoyance, ancient Egypt and pyramidology.

Anthony Aveni has noted that the spirit of medieval Gnosticism is present in 2012ology—and indeed the most energetic 2012 encyclopedist and marketer, an Englishman named Geoff Stray, names his website *2012: Dire Gnosis*. Central to Gnosticism, then and now, is both the belief in the magic of numbers—calculations and calendrics, formulas and codes—and the insistence that a mysterious, ancient, but crucial wisdom lies waiting to be uncovered.

Leaping ahead again—by another century—the Doomsday prophets were still at it, with 1975 being "pivotal" (as John Major Jenkins puts it) in 2012ology. Pyramidology resurfaced, but this time the focus was less on Egypt and more on Mexico and the Maya; books claimed to reveal the *Mexico Mystique* and the *Mysteries of the Mexican Pyramids*. This was the moment when the children of the 1960s first started using (more often, abusing) Maya calendrics, thereby laying the foundations for 2012ology. Postsixties counterculture appropriated the essence of older millenarian ideas; various imminent end-of-world dates were debated and proclaimed, until 2012 and the Maya mystique proved irresistible.

It was not only counterculture figures like José Arguelles and Terence McKenna who embraced the new millenarianism. In 1976, Pat Robertson predicted the world would end in 1982; in 1980 he repeated the prediction as "a guarantee" on his *700 Club* television show. Jerry Falwell explained to television audiences for decades that the Second Coming was almost upon us. Jack Van Impe, a fellow broadcast evangelist, is more specific: the end was to come in Y2K; now it is coming in 2012. Predictions that the world would end on specific dates during the 1980s and 1990s were made by a stream of published authors and preachers, among them Willie Day Smith, a Texan radio preacher; Chuck Smith, founder of the Calvary Chapel; and Branch Davidian leader David Koresh. When Edgar Whisenant's pamphlet *88 Reasons Why the Rapture Will Be in 1988* proved to be a disappointment, he quickly published a sequel, *The Final Shout: Rapture Report 1989.* He tried again in the 1990s, with each book's title updated accordingly.

It would be easy to dismiss all these prophets as kooks and criminals, and indeed some have gone to jail. For example, Rollen Stewart, famous for holding up "John 3:16" signs at sporting events, is now serving a life sentence for kidnapping, and Lee Jam Ring, founder of the Tami Church cult movement, was convicted of fraud. But the broadcasters find substantial audiences (the *700 Club* is still on the air), the book sales add up to the millions (*88 Reasons* alone sold over two million copies), and, like the Millerites in 1834, people are regularly convinced to sell their worldly goods and follow leaders to hilltops or (with the case of Elizabeth Clare Prophet in 1990) to a Montana ranch to await the end. The result can be tragic; thirty-nine members of the Heaven's Gate cult committed suicide in a house in San Diego in 1997, convinced by their apocalyptic leader Marshall Applewhite that it was the only way their souls could transport up to a waiting spaceship.

It was inevitable that various forms of millenarian hysteria would bubble to the surface in 1999; that Y2K panic focused on computer crashes was a sign and symbol of the difficult relationship between old traditions of Apocalypse and new cultures of technology. That tension surfaced again after Y2K in various ways.

One fascinating example is the brief, global media blitz produced in 2003 by the discovery of a couple of scraps of paper written by Isaac Newton around 1705. Both documents contained his calculations, based on his study of the Book of Revelation, which predicted that the world would end on or after 2060. How could one of the founding fathers of modern science, asked scandalized reporters, embrace apocalyptic prophecy? Then in 2008, when scientists in Switzerland switched on the new $8 billion supercollider, some feared it would spawn a black hole that would swallow up the earth. Newton is condemned, because he was a scientist, for taking Apocalypse seriously; but science itself is feared as the possible instrument of doom. The supercollider symbolizes how far the application of scientific principles, rather than blind faith, have taken—and might take—us. But the fears it provoked remind us of that other thread—Millerism, fear of a Martian invasion, 2012 hysteria—that still runs strong in our civilization.

~

How do the Maya fit into all this? Specifically, why has the notion that we can learn from ancient Maya wisdom had such popular appeal? The reasons are no doubt many, but we suggest four.

First of all, the popular perception of the Maya as mysterious is deeply rooted in our culture, going back at least as far as the 1840s, when John Lloyd Stephens's and Frederick Catherwood's travelogues and etchings of Maya cities uncovered by their intrepid expeditions into the jungle were best-sellers (figure 31 is an example; a "broken idol" at Copán). Since then, Maya studies has blossomed into a serious discipline, a major source of tourist revenue in four nations, a reference point for every genre of movie and book imaginable. In other words, the ancient Maya are an international industry, one whose beating heart is the idea that Maya civilization is a source of bottomless mystery and revelation. In short, mining the Maya for proof that 2012 "is real" is to draw on a long tradition of Mayanist imagination.

The New Age branch of 2012ologists claim to extract "secret wisdom from lost civilizations" (in Aveni's words). The Maya are not the sole such source, just the latest and greatest. The ancient Egyptians and the Incas have periodically received this kind of attention since

31. Frederick Catherwood, *Idol at Copan*, 1844.

the nineteenth century (as mentioned above)—Egypt experienced a massive spike in popularity in the years following the discovery of Tutankhamen's tomb in 1922, with King Tut's Curse a popular topic ever since; recent examples of modern Gnostic exposés carry titles such as *The Egypt Code* and *The Secret of the Incas*. The borderless, international purview of modern Gnosticism, combined with Western academia's "neocolonial" determination to discover and recover ancient places and peoples, has allowed us—our civilization—to claim Stonehenge, Giza, Tikal, Machu Picchu, and those who built them. For various reasons—foremost among them the recent boom in Mayanist epigraphy and archaeology—that gaze of appreciation and appropriation is fixated for now on the Maya.

The second reason why Maya Doomsday prophecy has had such modern appeal is—somewhat paradoxically its seemingly scientific dimension. The description of Maya knowledge as based on astronomy and complex mathematics makes it seem scientific, and thus, in a way, modern. In a world where science is often pitted against Christianity (think evolution vs. creationism), the lack of a Christian context to ancient texts such as the Tortuguero monument adds to the paradoxically modern aura of Maya wisdom. One cannot help being awed by the beautiful precision of a carved date like that of Cobá's Stela 1, seeming to calculate the age of the universe so many centuries before modern physicists were able to make a similar estimate. The impression given by such calculations is that the ancient Maya were accomplished scientists a millennium or two before the West's scientific revolution even began.

A third—and closely related—explanation is the connection between the Maya calendar and astronomy. We have already discussed earlier the possibility that the Maya knew of the precession and debunked the idea that they could have known with any precision at all when it would occur—let alone predicted that the earth, sun, and the Milky Way would align in 2012. As Aveni concludes (and he has examined the topic in great detail), "it is likely that the Maya knew that what we call 'precession' existed, but to date there is no evidence to support the case that they calculated the cycle, much less even perceived precession as a cyclic phenomenon." Even if it were possible for the Maya to know this—and it is not possible—there is no such alignment taking place specifically in 2012, let alone on December 21. The alignment—that is, "the sun at winter solstice crossing the plane of the Milky Way Galaxy"—will occur during this century or the next, or perhaps the one after. And when it does, there is no evidence at all that it will have an impact on earth. That, of course, has not stopped numerous 2012 prophets from predicting a wide array of events that will result, from global destruction to a mass spiritual awakening.

More to the point here, such predictions are part of a larger phenomenon of astronomical millenarianism. These range from the relatively sober, such as anxiety over sun spots, to the hysterical, such as the Planet X theory. Every eleven years dark spots appear on the surface of the sun, caused by plasma eruptions. These eruptions produce magnetic fields and solar storms, but at worst they damage or disrupt satellites and at best they cause stunningly beautiful auroras. The sun spot cycle will approach a peak in 2012–2013. This is cited as further evidence of a major cosmic occurrence. But sun spot activity will be modest (it was heavier in 1980 and 1990–1991), it will not climax on a specific day or even month, and there is no reason to believe that its minuscule impact on us will be any different from all the previous eleven-year peaks.

The Planet X theory claims that the ancient Sumerians predicted that a planet called Nibiru (aka X) would collide with earth in 2012. Needless to say, there was no such prediction and there is no such planet. On the other hand, there are asteroids and comets moving through space, and some have hit us. This simple fact has fueled fears that—Nibiru aside—an asteroid will strike earth in 2012 and wipe us all out, just as the massive impact of an asteroid sixty-five million years ago appears to have wiped out the dinosaurs.

This speculation takes us back to—you guessed it—the Maya. The impact point of that asteroid (depicted in figure 32) is called the

32. Donald E. Davis, *Meteor Hitting the Earth and Creating the Chicxulub Crater.*

Chicxulub Crater, because a massive asteroid chunk called the Baptistina fragment hit the northern Yucatan peninsula right where the Maya fishing village of Chicxulub would later stand. Of course, the time span between the asteroid impact and the formation of Maya settlements in Yucatan was—well, about sixty-five million years. And by then the crater was buried deep underground and under the Gulf of Mexico, invisible and unknown to us until oil company geophysicists discovered it in 1978. But to some the coincidence is no coincidence at all; the Maya knew when the next global Apocalypse would come from the sky because they lived on top of the place where the last one happened.

The fourth explanation we suggest for why the Maya seem to make such good prophets of doom is part of a larger point about how we see Apocalypse—literally, see it. To be sure, depictions of Apocalypse over the centuries have been multifaceted, containing many textual and oral dimensions (as discussed earlier). But we contend that above all, the end of the world has been conceived and perceived in visual terms. In the West, that visual dimension runs from medieval depictions of doom and the grim etchings of Dürer to the man with the sandwich board proclaiming "The End Is Nigh" and the crumbling cities in the movie *2012* (see figure 33).

Scholars of medieval Europe have argued that the concept of the Apocalypse became so powerful because of "its dramatically symbolic mode of communication"; the final struggle between good and evil

33. Promotional postcard for *2012*, Sony Pictures, 2009.

is conveyed through a wide range of symbolic opposites—such as the Four Horsemen vs. the Seven Angels—that are easy to grasp and boggle the mind. These symbols were also highly visual, and increasingly so in the late-medieval and early modern centuries, as illustrated by the images in the previous three chapters. Here is another example (figure 34, a thirteenth-century Anglo-Norman depiction of the Apocalypse drawn to accompany excerpts from the Book of Revelation). The image of tumbling city buildings as a symbol of the civilized life, the world we have built, destroyed in an instant, is powerful because of its immediate visual impact. Our point is not that there is a direct line of influence from medieval manuscripts (figure 34) to Hollywood (figure 33) (although there is a larger point implied regarding the persistence of apocalyptic notions in the West), but rather that in our civilization the end of the world has for many centuries been something we *see*.

The visual nature of Maya prophecies is vivid and obvious. Even the ancient Maya texts that contribute to the myth of 2012 predictions take the form of visually impressive hieroglyphs. For centuries nobody could read these glyphs, and even today they are legible only to a small number of Mayanist epigraphers. Furthermore, as we saw earlier, the translated texts remain esoteric, their apocalyptic meanings obscure and dependent upon lengthy and imaginative explanations. As a result, their larger impact is as image, not word—it is visual rather than textual. Those who have insisted on the Maya origins and foundations of 2012 draw attention to memorable motifs, not phrases—carved glyphic dates, the layout of spectacular monumental buildings, a galactic map in the form of a tree, bird, alligator, and warrior—and they are quick to appropriate visual imagery from other places, such as the Aztec Calendar Stone. Maya (or Aztec) sources shore up 2012ology not because of what they say but because of what they seem to show.

∽

What if the ancient Maya were not as good at astrology and calendrical mathematics as we think they were? What if we are not as good

34. *The Apocalypse*, from Manuscript 524 of the Morgan Group Manuscripts.

at interpreting Maya knowledge as we think we are? What if, in other words, December 21, 2012, comes as a huge anticlimax—but the world still comes to an end, without warning, on another day?

This is certainly what many believe, and there is no shortage of alternative dates. Some come before 2012 and may have passed uneventfully, you will be happy to hear, by the time you are reading these words. For example, a church group in Oakland, California, distributed pamphlets in much of the United States in 2010 warning that the world would end on May 21, 2011. Carl-Johann Calleman, a contributor to the New Age branch of 2012ology whose book on the Maya calendar was titled *Solving the Greatest Mystery of Our Time*, argues that 2012 is a misreading; the real end date is October 21, 2011, when we shall all have the opportunity to enter the Universal Underworld of Consciousness.

Other predictions pick dates after 2012, typically drawing upon the imagined wisdom of cultures other than the Maya (who—and here is *our* prediction—will immediately fall out of favor in 2013 for their failure to get it right). As we saw in chapter 4, the Aztec Calendar Stone is often taken to be a guide to the cycle that ends with Apocalypse. One such interpretation—which seems to teeter on the fence between absurdity and outright parody—claims that by adapting the stone's design so it can be placed on a compact disc, one can play the CD backward and hear plans for an invasion of the earth by Reticulan aliens on July 8, 2022. Another claims that the Calendar Stone is "properly called the Eagle Bowl" and that its prediction of the Apocalypse can be decoded using a Zapotec prophecy; in one variant, that prophecy is inscribed in Zapotec on a bone, warning us that the end is coming in September 2017.

It doesn't matter whether the year is 2017, 2022, or 2060, or whether the source is Aztec, Zapotec, or Isaac Newton—or *XX Reasons Why the Rapture Will Be in 20XX* (you be the prophet). Because in the end, the 2012 phenomenon is not ultimately about the year 2012, or about the Maya. It is about the apocalyptic impulse that lies deep within our civilization. Many positive things can come from

2012—be it a greater interest in the ancient Maya and other past civilizations, or be it an infusion of interest in such concepts as spiritual awakening and global harmony. But 2012 is not the end; it is merely a stepping stone on the millenarian pathway that is likely to persist for another . . . well, let's say, thousand years.

Sources and Suggestions
for Further Reading

$\mathcal{T}$he first translation of the Tortuguero Monument 6 text was published by Stephen D. Houston and David Stuart, "Of Gods, Glyphs, and Kings: Divinity and Rulership among the Classic Maya," *Antiquity* 70 (1996): 289–312. There are further comments by Houston, Stuart, and others on the text at the Maya Decipherment blog (decipherment.wordpress.com). The most recent and comprehensive treatment of the text is by Sven Gronemeyer and Barbara MacLeod, "What Could Happen in 2012: A Re-Analysis of the 13-*Bak'tun* Prophecy on Tortuguero Monument 6," in *Wayeb Notes* #34 (2010), available at wayeb.org.

The literature on the ancient Maya is copious, so the following works are by no means the only fine studies. An excellent survey that briefly details all aspects of Maya life, while also deftly summarizing the debates among Mayanists, is Stephen Houston and Takeshi Inomata, *The Classic Maya* (Cambridge, 2009). On the decipherment of Maya writing, we recommend Michael Coe's *Breaking the Maya Code* (Thames & Hudson, 1992), and on the political history that the glyphs record, Simon Martin and Nikolai Grube, *Chronicle of Maya Kings and Queens* (Thames & Hudson, 2000). On Maya art, see the various books by Mary Miller. In our opinion, the best study of the "collapse" period in Maya history is by our Penn State colleague, David Webster, *The Fall of the Ancient Maya: Solving the Mystery of the Maya Collapse* (Thames & Hudson, 2002). On the calendar, see Prudence M. Rice, *Maya Calendar Origins: Monuments, Mythistory, and the Materialization of Time* (University of Texas Press, 2007).

On Copán and Quiriguá, two excellent books by leading Mayanists are William L. Fash, *Scribes, Warriors and Kings: The City of Copán and the Ancient Maya* (Thames & Hudson, 1991) and Matthew Looper, *Lightning Warrior: Maya Art and Kingship at Quirigua* (University of Texas Press, 2003).

The John Major Jenkins quote is from his alignment2012.com website, but also see his various books, such as *The 2012 Story: The Myths, Fallacies, and Truth behind the Most Intriguing Date in History* (Tarcher/Penguin, 2009). Jenkins is not a professional academic, he rails against such scholars, and he often ignores the basic rules of evidence and argument followed by Mayanists. However, he is in a different league from other nonacademic 2012 writers; he is prolific yet writes engagingly and often persuasively, he exhibits a profound and passionate appreciation and respect for Maya culture, and above all he is well intentioned, condemning the scaremongers and insisting that 2012 will bring positive changes.

We suggest that readers interested in moving on to additional books about the 2012 phenomenon consider Jenkins's *The 2012 Story* for the perspectives of 2012ology, and Anthony Aveni's *The End of Time: The Maya Mystery of 2012* (University Press of Colorado, 2009) for an accessible yet scholarly exploration of the ways in which Maya calendrics and astronomy have been misunderstood.

Unless otherwise noted, the transcriptions and translations from the *Books of Chilam Balam* are our own, made from the original manuscripts. The Edmonson and Bricker quote is from their *Supplement Volume 3: Literatures* to the *Handbook of Middle American Indians* (University of Texas Press), p. 51; and the Edmonson quotes are from his *Heaven Born Merida and Its Destiny: The Book of Chilam Balam of Chu-*

mayel (University of Texas Press, 1986), pp. 44, 153. Full translations of the *Chumayel* were made by Ralph L. Roys in 1933 (University of Oklahoma Press edition, 1967), of the *Tizimin* and *Chumayel* by Munro Edmonson in the 1980s (both University of Texas Press), and most recently of the *Chumayel* by Richard Luxton (Aegean Park Press, 1995).

The quote from Landa can be found in any edition of his *Relación de las cosas de Yucatán* (e.g., Dastin, 2002, p. 115).

CHAPTER 2

The quotes at the top of the chapter are by Dennis Overbye, "Is Doomsday Coming? Perhaps, but Not in 2012," *New York Times*, November 16, 2009 (accessed at http://www.nytimes.com/2009/11/17/science/17essay.html); and from Jenkins, *The 2012 Story*, p. 60.

The placing of the Tortuguero text in the context of Naranjo and La Corona is from Stephen Houston's comments posted on the Maya Decipherment blog (decipherment.wordpress.com). For a more detailed discussion of the Palenque glyphs, see Linda Schele and David Freidel, *A Forest of Kings: The Untold Story of the Ancient Maya* (Morrow, 1990), especially pp. 237–61.

Stephen Jay Gould's witty little book on Y2K is *Questioning the Millennium: A Rationalist's Guide to a Precisely Arbitrary Countdown* (Harmony, 1997).

The quote by Mary Ellen Miller is from p. 8 of her *Maya Art and Architecture* (Thames & Hudson, 1999). The Makemson essay was published as "The Miscellaneous Dates of the Dresden Codex," in *Publications of the Vassar College Observatory* 6:4 (June 1957); it is available online. Coe's *The Maya* has been published by Thames & Hudson since 1966. Our tracking of comments on 2012 by Makemson, Coe, and others was assisted by similar summaries by Jenkins, *The 2012 Story*, pp. 56–57, and in the "2012 phenomenon" entry on Wikipedia.

The discussion on precession includes quotes by Jenkins from *The 2012 Story*, p. 215, and by Aveni from *The End of Time*, pp. 100–106. The Jenkins quotes are from his alignment2012.com website and from *The 2012 Story*, his discussion of Tortuguero on pp. 217–23. The Aveni references are taken from his essay "Apocalypse Soon?" in *Archaeology* 62:6 (2009), at archaeology.org. The Tedlock quote is from Dennis Tedlock, *2000 Years of Mayan Literature* (University of California Press, 2010), p. 136. Our discussion of the calendar draws on Tedlock's book and on Rice's *Maya Calendar Origins*.

CHAPTER 3

The quotes of speech by Nebuchadnezzar are from Daniel 2:5, 2:6, and 2:31–35; the Jesus reference to Daniel is in Matthew 24. The quote by Fernández-Armesto is from his *1492: The Year the World Began* (HarperOne, 2009), p. 144, with the Savonarola quotes taken from the same book, p. 127. The Rule of St. Francis of Assissi is reproduced widely and easily found online. The "venerable historian" quote is by John Leddy Phelan, *The Millennial Kingdom of the Franciscans in the New World: A Study of the Writings of Gerónimo de Mendieta (1525–1604)* (University of California, 1956), p. 1.

There is a vast scholarly literature on early Christianity, medieval European religious history, and all things to do with the history of millenarianism in Mediterranean and Western civilization—including a hefty, dense, three-volume *Encyclopedia of Apocalypticism* (Continuum, 2000). Many books attempt to be both accessible and scholarly, among them Nicholas Campion, *The Great Year: Astrology, Millenarianism, and History in the Western Tradition* (Arkana, 1994), and Jonathan Kirsch, *A History of the End of the World: How the Most Controversial Book in the Bible Changed the Course of Western Civilization* (Harper San Francisco, 2006). A fine starting point for Franciscan history is *The Franciscan Story: St. Francis of Assisi and His Influence since the Thirteenth Century* (Athena, 2008) by Maurice Carmody, himself a member of the order.

CHAPTER 4

The quote from Cortés is our translation from his second letter; see the original Spanish in Hernán Cortés, *Cartas de Relación* (Porrúa, 1983), p. 52; for the full passage in English, see Anthony Pagden, ed., Hernán Cortés, *Letters from Mexico* (Yale, 1986), pp. 85–86. Our quotes from Barbara Tuchman are from *The March of Folly: From Troy to Vietnam* (Ballantine, 1984), pp. 13, 383. The Jared Diamond quote is from *Guns, Germs, and Steel: The Fates of Human Societies* (Norton, 1997), p. 80. The excerpts from the Florentine Codex are based on the definitive translation by James Lockhart, in *We People Here: Nahuatl Accounts of the Conquest of Mexico* (University of California Press, 1993), p. 116.

The Vespucci quote is from Felipe Fernández-Armesto's *Amerigo: The Man Who Gave His Name to America* (Random House, 2007), p. 121. The phrases from Luke are 14:21 and 14:24. For an excellent overview of the apocalyptic nature of Mendieta's writings, see Phelan's *Millennial Kingdom*, cited earlier; the quotes in this chapter are from pp. 6, 8. The quotes from the native annals are in Camilla Townsend, *Here in This Year: Seventeenth-Century Nahuatl Annals of the Tlaxcala-Puebla Valley* (Stanford, 2010), using the transcriptions and translations by Townsend and James Lockhart, pp. 69, 159, 161.

There is an extensive literature by historians, anthropologists, and other scholars on early colonial Mexico and the Spiritual Conquest; in addition to Lockhart, Phelan, and Townsend, noteworthy contributors include Louise Burkhart, Mark Christensen, Serge Gruzinski, Max Harris, Robert Haskett, Jeanette Peterson, John F. Schwaller, and Stephanie Wood. For further discussion of the arguments we make about Moctezuma and Cortés, see Matthew Restall, *Seven Myths of the Spanish Conquest* (Oxford, 2003).

CHAPTER 5

On the *Books of Chilam Balam*—the original texts, translations, and the analysis by Edmonson and others—see our comments on chapter 3's sources. The quotes from Cruzob Maya rebels are taken from Victoria Reifler Bricker, *The Indian Christ, the Indian King: The Historical Substrate of Maya Myth and Ritual* (University of Texas Press, 1981), pp. 104, 108.

There is a fine recent body of scholarly works on colonial and nineteenth-century Yucatan, from the Spanish invasions through the Caste War; in addition to Bricker and the authors of this book (our work focuses primarily on Yucatan), notable contributors include John Chuchiak, Inga Clendinnen, Don Dumond, Samuel Edgerton, Wolfgang Gabbert, William F. Hanks, Craig A. Hanson, Grant D. Jones, Robert Patch, Terry Rugeley, Pete Sigal, and Paul Sullivan. Those authors cite a further fine body of work published in Spanish.

CHAPTER 6

DuPlooy's Jungle Lodge website is www.duplooys.com/index.php. Articles on other predictions include Marcelo Gleiser, "2012: The Year the World Will Not End" (May 11, 2010) on the NPR website at http://www.npr.org/blogs/13.7/2010/03/2012_the_year_the_world_will_en.html; and a hilarious piece by Chris Wright: "Alternative Endings" (November 22, 2009), in the *Boston Globe*, available at http://www.boston.com/bostonglobe/ideas/articles/2009/11/22/alternate_endings_what_if_the_world_doesnt_end_in_2012/.

The many books of Michael Shermer are easily found at booksellers or libraries. The quote by him is taken from a review by Robert T. Carroll of Shermer's *Why People Believe Weird Things: Pseudoscience, Superstition, and Other Confusions of Our Time* (Freeman & Co., 1997), at http://www.skepdic.com/refuge/weird.html. The Newton quote at the top of the chapter, and our discussion of Newton that follows, is taken from a fine essay by Stephen Snobelen at www.isaac-newton.org/newton_2060.htm.

The history of "revitalization" movements is explored and placed in millenarian contexts by Michael E. Harkin, ed., *Reassessing Revitalization Movements* (University of Nebraska Press, 2004); his introduction was especially useful to us.

The fanzine *The End Is Nigh* can be found at www.endisnigh .co.uk. There are a number of studies of the 1938 Wells/Welles broadcast, a recent one being John Gosling's *Waging the War of the Worlds: A History of the 1938 Radio Broadcast and Resulting Panic* (MacFarland, 2009). Jenkins offers an engaging and witty interpretation of the origins of 2012ology—and one that is notably objective considering his personal involvement in the movement—in *The 2012 Story,* pp. 82–121; pp. 124 and 218 contain his "closed shop," etc., phrases. Stray's *2012: Dire Gnosis* website is at www.diagnosis2012. co.uk/. A lively dissection of alternative imaginings of the ancient past is Garrett G. Fagan, ed., *Archaeological Fantasies: How Pseudoarchaeology Misrepresents the Past and Misleads the Public* (Routledge, 2006). The "mode of communication" quote is by Bernard McGinn in Richard Emmerson and McGinn, eds., *The Apocalypse in the Middle Ages* (Cornell, 1992), p. 16. The Aveni quotes on precession are in his *The End of Time,* pp. 106, 115.

Index

About the Authors

Matthew Restall and **Amara Solari** are specialists in Maya culture and colonial Mexican history. Between them they have over thirty years of experience studying Mayan languages and researching the Maya past in the towns and archives of Mexico, Central America, and Spain. Their knowledge of Yucatec Maya gives them the rare ability to decipher the original Maya texts. Both teach at the Pennsylvania State University. Restall is Edwin Erle Sparks Professor of Latin American History and Anthropology and has published over a dozen books, including *Maya Conquistador* and *Seven Myths of the Spanish Conquest*. Solari is assistant professor of art history and anthropology, has published articles on colonial Maya mapping systems, and has written a book on Itzmal, Yucatan.